THE ART OF Connection
How to Get Along With Anyone Anywhere

THE ART OF CONNECTION
HOW TO GET ALONG WITH ANYONE ANYWHERE

© 2025 Brandon K. Moore

All rights reserved. No part of this publication may be reproduced, distributed, or transmitted in any form or by any means, including photocopying, recording, or other electronic or mechanical methods, without the prior written permission of the publisher, except in the case of brief quotations embodied in critical reviews and certain other noncommercial uses permitted by copyright law. For permission requests, please contact the author.

Published by BKM Publishing | Argyle, Texas

ISBN (Paperback): 978-1-957812-10-6

ISBN (EPUB): 978-1-957812-09-0

ISBN: (Audiobook): 978-1-957812-11-3

Library of Congress Control Number (LCCN): 2025915030

Printed in the United States of America

Prepared for Publication by: wendykwalters.com

Scripture quotations marked ESV are taken from The Holy Bible, English Standard Version. ESV® Text Edition: 2016. Copyright © 2001 by Crossway Bibles, a publishing ministry of Good News Publishers.

Scripture quotations marked NIV are taken from the Holy Bible, New International Version®, NIV® Copyright ©1973, 1978, 1984, 2011 by Biblica, Inc.® Used by permission. All rights reserved worldwide.

Scripture quotations marked NKJV are taken from the New King James Version®. Copyright © 1982 by Thomas Nelson. Used by permission. All rights reserved.

Scripture quotations marked NLT are taken from the Holy Bible, New Living Translation, copyright © 1996, 2004, 2015 by Tyndale House Foundation. Used by permission of Tyndale House Publishers, Inc., Carol Stream, Illinois 60188. All rights reserved.

Scripture quotations marked MSG are taken from THE MESSAGE, copyright © 1993, 2002, 2018 by Eugene H. Peterson. Used by permission of NavPress. All rights reserved. Represented by Tyndale House Publishers, Inc.

Scripture quotations marked TPT are from The Passion Translation®. Copyright © 2017, 2018, 2020 by Passion & Fire Ministries, Inc. Used by permission. All rights reserved. ThePassionTranslation.com.

To contact the author:

BRANDONKMOORE.COM

DEDICATION

To Angela, Kate and Ryan, Conner and Emily, Ian and Paris, Sutton and his future wife—

You are the reason I charge my soul to become a better man. Because you deserve it!

PRAISE FOR THE ART OF CONNECTION

I am amazed by the transparency by which Brandon wrote this book and the practical life applications he has presented throughout. Lessons learned and wisdom gained from other's experiences is like finding precious gems on the surface that others spent years digging for. Grounded in scripture and filled with thoughtful insight and spiritual wisdom, this book will equip you to be successful in life. I am encouraged and immensely grateful that my friend Brandon Moore wrote this book, and I know you will be too.

DR. ABRAHAM MATHEW, CPA
Founder and President, Southern Asia Leadership Institute

Brandon's latest book is an honest look at what goes wrong when forging relationships and is full of reminders of things we (should) already know when attempting to build lasting bonds with our friends and family members. Reading this book can help you cultivate mindfulness as you observe the relationships around you.

MAGGIE DANIEL
Director of Marketing, Local CPA Firm

The Art of Connection beautifully weaves timeless relational wisdom with biblical truth, offering readers a Christ-centered path to stronger, healthier connections. I found myself wanting to put this book into the hands of my adult children, newly married couples, and parents of young children to help them avoid the pitfalls and pain that come from poor communication. Brandon Moore reminds us that getting along isn't about pleasing people: it's about reflecting the heart of God in how we listen, speak, and love.

WENDY K. WALTERS
Vice President of ISM Publishing

THE ART OF CONNECTION

CONTENTS

CHAPTER ONE — 11
UNLOCK YOUR SOCIAL SUPERPOWER

CHAPTER TWO — 19
WHAT IT MEANS TO GET ALONG

CHAPTER THREE — 35
AVOID THE POISON OF CRITICISM

CHAPTER FOUR — 49
PRAISE FREELY

CHAPTER FIVE — 67
EXPRESS APPRECIATION DAILY

CHAPTER SIX — 85
FORGIVE QUICKLY

CHAPTER SEVEN — 105
LEARN TO LISTEN

CHAPTER EIGHT — 127
ASK CURIOUS QUESTIONS

CHAPTER NINE — 145
SET HEALTHY BOUNDARIES

CHAPTER TEN — 161
THE END ... AND THE REAL BEGINNING

THE ART OF CONNECTION

CHAPTER ONE

UNLOCK YOUR SOCIAL SUPERPOWER

What if I told you that it was possible to get along with anyone? I mean, even the really difficult people. What if you could crack the code on how to communicate effectively to de-escalate tense situations, ensure that you understand others and are understood by them, learn how to confront inappropriate behavior, establish rapport, and grow respect with every person in your life?

Imagine how your relationships would change. Think about how this ability to get along with anyone, anywhere, could impact your professional success as well as your personal fulfillment.

Would that interest you?

It certainly interests me. The reason I wrote this book was to help others avoid all the pitfalls I fell into. I care about this subject so much because, for most of my life, I pretty much did the opposite of everything you need to do to get along well with others. Once I became aware of how my beliefs and behavior impacted my ability to get along with others, I went on a long journey to discover and develop the tools I needed to have the kind of rapport and relationships I always longed for but always seemed to blow up.

That doesn't have to be your story.

ORIGINS

Superhero origin stories are everywhere—crash-landing from a distant planet, being bitten by a radioactive spider, or witnessing a tragedy. Sure, we love their powers, but we long to know where they came from and what shaped them. It helps us relate to them. So, while I can't manipulate lightning or shoot webs (yet), I do have an origin story of my own to share with you.

I grew up in Irving, Texas, in the eighties. It was, at the time, the divorce capital of the world. More than fifty percent of marriages at that time ended in divorce. It was a depressing statistic and a first for our country. The 1980s marked the decline of marriage, and it hasn't rebounded since.

One Sunday, after my parents had just separated, my dad was dropping me off from his weekend with the kids. On this rare occasion, I was in the front seat. My dad parked on the street in front of our once-shared family home. My mother came out of the house looking angry and sad all at the same time. She stepped into the street, opened the car door, and grabbed my arm. I was eleven at the time. My dad said something about wanting me to go to his church that morning. That set my mother off into an angry rant about how I would go to her church as I had done my entire life. My dad then grabbed my other arm and tried to pull me back into the car, yelling at her that it was still his weekend, and I was going to his church.

I don't even remember why we were there, maybe to drop my brother off so he could go to my mom's church. He was older and always seemed to get to make his own choices. I don't remember what happened next. My brain escaped the trauma of the moment by checking out. I have no idea whose church I went to that day, but I vividly remember the tug-of-war that happened that morning and wanting to cry, yell, punch, and kick. But I did nothing. I wonder if our neighbors saw this shouting match with me as the rope in the middle.

I was ten years old when my parents separated. Insecure, confused, and sad, my world was turned into the now cliché "broken home." I spent every other weekend with my dad. Both my older brother and I lived with my mom, and we were shuffled between them like pets. The world I knew before the divorce wasn't great. My parents were both physically and mentally abusive to us. For years, I thought that our home was normal, though, because I didn't know any other kind of home existed. Sure, my dad spanked us, but it couldn't be abuse, right?

Let me tell you, there's a difference between spankings and what my dad did to us in fits of rage.

By the time of the separation, most of the "spankings" had ceased unless my dad got extremely angry. But the mental abuse didn't stop. My mother spent most of her days crying in her bedroom, loud enough for my brother and me to hear. She had made a list of the things my dad had "done to her" in a spiral notebook and then left it out for us to see and read. After blaming the devil for this souring relationship, my dad tried to become a loving father. Constantly, he would tell us he could provide more for us if we would just come to live with him (and by the way that would have reduced his child support payments).

I tell you this not for you to feel sorry for me. Some of you may have had a similar home life and have chosen, like me, not to be a victim. I tell you this story to give you the background of the kid I once was who had no voice. Every sentence, it seemed to me, from my parents and even my brother, dripped with criticism and doubt.

That's the learned behavior I took into my adulthood. Criticism, sarcasm, doubt, and failure were baked into my language. The way I related to people, constantly comparing and sizing them up. No one was good enough because I wasn't good enough.

But that's not how God relates to us. He speaks life to us. He loves us and values us just as we are. He wants us to become his children by accepting Jesus as Lord and then living from that identity.

My life was full of broken relationship after broken relationship, even after I became a born-again Christian. After becoming a believer, I still struggled with relationships. And I still struggle, but in the last few years, things have begun to change.

WORK IN PROGRESS

In 2017, my oldest son ran away from home.

Writing that sentence still causes adrenaline to rush through my body. I taste something bitter in the back of my mouth. My heartbeat quickens. My breathing comes quick and shallow. Sharing this moment with you makes me feel vulnerable—exposed. Equal parts of willingness to be real and the instinct to protect and cover. Why would I share something so personal and painful with you?

Because this event served as one of many catalysts for everything I am about to reveal in this book.

When my son ran away, it wasn't a stunt. He was gone for days. We had fought about him not wanting to go to school. I yelled. I shamed him. I criticized him—I said terrible things, and then my son walked out of our house.

At first, I thought he'd be back that night, and then the real argument would begin. I sort of geared up for it. I prepped like a lawyer ready to defend a case … but he didn't come home. After days away, I cried and pleaded with God. His mother lay awake every night waiting, hoping he'd come home. We finally received word that he was staying with some friends—boys who had graduated a year earlier. I confess it was during this failure in parenting that I began to see myself more clearly.

Knowing firsthand the damage this behavior could cause, I wondered: *How could I have become such a source of criticism and judgment in his life?*

Even now, it hurts to think about how much he and our other kids had to endure from me. I was supposed to be a source of hope and encouragement. Instead, I made them want to leave home. By my words and actions, I had caused them to feel as though they could never measure up.

Eventually, my son came home. I wish I could say I acted differently, but I'm not sure that I did. I think I showed him grace and love, but looking back, I know criticism came out without effort. I didn't yet

THE ART OF CONNECTION

know how to encourage. I had not developed the skills to allow the Holy Spirit to work in me so I could show him and others how much I loved them.

But that event stayed with me.

Haunted me.

It was the kind of watershed moment that made me assess everything and divide it into before and after. I decided then that I would learn to do things differently—I had to do things differently. If I truly loved my family, if I truly wanted to be the man God had created me to be, it was time for me to look hard in the mirror and figure out what I was lacking. It was time I allowed the Lord to identify my issues so the Holy Spirit could begin to fill in the gaps.

> IT WAS TIME FOR ME TO LOOK HARD IN THE MIRROR AND FIGURE OUT WHAT I WAS LACKING.

Thus, I began a journey of self-awareness and freedom. I became more aware of the behavior that turned people away. I also began to learn to stop trying to please everyone. Some of the things I have learned, I hope to share with you.

The title of this book is bold. I know. It's meant to grab your attention and give you hope. But what I don't want is for you to think that it all depends on you. God is with you. He is already pleased with you. He will never leave you or forsake you. But He has given us so many tools to use to be able to love others as we love ourselves that there is no reason we can't live in harmony with others and experience fruitful relationships.

UNLOCK YOUR SOCIAL SUPERPOWER

You may be like me and have a wake of broken relationships behind you. You may be like my wife and have a long list of people who have taken advantage of your kindness and hurt you. You may have a large friend group and don't understand why some of them are friends with you but not with each other. Relationships are hard. They can be so rewarding yet have such a great risk to your emotional well-being.

This book can help you navigate those relationships. From learning what not to say to learning how to be someone others want to be around. Nothing in the book is new. However, putting it together and applying it to our relationships will help us grow emotionally and spiritually.

After reading this book, I hope that you will be ready to approach new relationships and deepen the ones you have. It is difficult to be vulnerable and let people in, yet that is the only way to build trust and connect with people.

I have been on this journey for years now. As a business owner, husband, father, pastor, and friend, I have found these truths change the way I interact with people and transform the relationship. When you incorporate these principles into your life, people will want to be around you. They will seek you out when they need a friend, want to hang out, or just need to talk.

I'm surprised every day how negative people can be in our world when Jesus said, "The words I speak to you, they are life."[1] At its heart, this book is about connection—how to create it, protect it, and grow through it. Whether you are navigating everyday routine conversations or dealing with stressful or intense situations, the principles here are designed to help you show up with clarity, compassion, and confidence.

By understanding others more deeply—and yourself more honestly—you'll learn to build relationships rooted in mutual respect, meaningful dialogue, and healthy boundaries. While this book is about helping you get along with others, it is even more about growing together. So, let's learn together how to speak words of life to each other. Let's learn to have meaningful conversations.

ENDNOTE

1. See John 6:63 (paraphrased).

CHAPTER TWO

WHAT IT MEANS TO GET ALONG

GETTING ALONG

What does it mean to get along with others? Does it require that we live passively, allowing others to walk all over us? Must we sacrifice our identity or our agency to keep the peace? I don't think so. To get along with others isn't totally on us—is it? You are not responsible for the mood or behavior of others. Just as God gave us free will and does not impose His will over ours, we cannot change other people's behavior. However, in the same way that God can influence us to cultivate a relationship with Him, to move toward repentance, or to awaken to a flaw in our character, we can influence others through our desire for peace.

Paul said it this way:

> *"If it is possible, as much as depends on you, live peaceably with all men."*
>
> ROMANS 12:18, NKJV

THE ART OF CONNECTION

This puts some responsibility on us. "As much as depends on you …." That is an eye-opening statement. I know I have read that a hundred times. But something jumped out at me a few weeks before writing this book began. I realized that I have a responsibility to live in peace with others. This revelation led me to think about how that translates into real life. As I stated in the introduction, I had been an arrogant, self-centered, judgmental jerk for the first forty years of my life (maybe more), and I have been on a journey of personal improvement for some time. I'm not finished working on being a better human—a different human, one who is more Christ-like and a lot closer to the original design He created. But one of the biggest parts of learning to change was to acknowledge and accept that I had a responsibility in the chaos of my previous relationships.

I once worked for a CPA who had a bookkeeper/office manager whom I did not get along with. She had such an overbearing personality. She wanted to control every aspect of the office, and my boss let her. That angered me. I took it upon myself to help her understand that she wasn't in charge. Whenever I could, I questioned her and what she was doing. When she told me to do something (usually relaying what my boss wanted as a command), I did my best to question the direction. Well, it didn't take long until the boss handed me a severance check. It was December 22, 2000. Three days before Christmas. I had two kids, a wife to support, and no job. My arrogance and self-importance helped me become part of the unemployed.

Unfortunately, I didn't learn from that experience. For a long time, I believed I was a victim. I presumed I had lost that job because the boss found out I was looking elsewhere, which only fueled my victim belief. Maybe it would have ended differently if I had been a different

WHAT IT MEANS TO GET ALONG

person. One who was grateful for the job and who would accept my role and the role others had in the office.

WHO DO WE NEED TO GET ALONG WITH?

This question is easy to answer but more difficult to manage. Of course, we need to get along with friends, family, and coworkers. But what about when those relationships are unhealthy? Do we need to stay in toxic relationships? What if those relationships are with our family members?

Stay with me for a moment and look at this passage in Luke for insight into how to deal with toxic relationships:

> *But whatever house you enter, first say, "Peace to this house." And if a son of peace is there, your peace will rest on it; if not, it will return to you. And remain in the same house, eating and drinking such things as they give, for the laborer is worthy of his wages. Do not go from house to house.*
>
> *Whatever city you enter, and they receive you, eat such things as are set before you. And heal the sick there, and say to them, "The kingdom of God has come near to you." But whatever city you enter, and they do not receive you, go out into its streets and say, "The very dust of your city which clings to us we wipe off against you. Nevertheless know this, that the kingdom of God has come near you."*
>
> LUKE 10:5-11, NKJV

THE ART OF CONNECTION

First, Luke tells us to seek people of peace, "If a son of peace is there, your peace will rest on it…" So is that saying when we go through our day, we are supposed to deal only with "sons of peace"? It would be great if we could just avoid anyone that we didn't like—bosses, siblings, parents. But unfortunately, that isn't really possible. Jesus tells us that if the people we encounter aren't sons of peace, our peace will return to us. I admit that didn't make much sense to me.

But then I began to think about how God led me when I had a person I worked with whom I didn't much care for. Guess what? He was one of the staff pastors at a church I not only attended but worked for. Another pastor told me, "You can love people without liking them. Just because you work with them (or they are pastors/leaders) doesn't mean you have to hang out with them." Now, I see the passage in Luke as a guide to how much energy and effort I should put into relationships. If someone isn't a person of peace, why waste energy trying to get along with them? Why use up your peace on someone who couldn't care less about you? You may not be able to change how much time you work with them or interact with them, but there is something freeing about not letting them take your peace. We will get into setting healthy boundaries in a later chapter, but not allowing someone to take your peace is one of those ways to set a healthy boundary.

In my previous books, I discussed my parents and how they have not been good people. They have been angry, judgmental, and critical their whole lives. For a time, I had to stop allowing them to take my peace. For the sake of my marriage and my children, I had to cut them off from visiting or calling. I love my parents. But I don't like being around them. Their negative life filter makes conversations difficult to get through. You may have family members who are takers and not givers. They may be jealous of your accomplishments

WHAT IT MEANS TO GET ALONG

or just nasty people. You don't have to spend your energy on them at the expense of your family. Until you are strong enough to maintain your joy and peace and be around them, don't let them into your inner circle. Protect that circle—and don't just take my word for it. Listen to Solomon:

> *"Keep your heart with all diligence, for out of it spring the issues of life."*
>
> PROVERBS 4:23, NKJV

Getting along also means that you don't let people bully or verbally abuse you. Getting along may mean that you walk away from those people while they are forming the next sentence. Just because you want to "live peaceably with one another" doesn't mean that you become someone's verbal punching bag. The Bible tells us to avoid evil and cling to what is good.[1] It also tells us to think on things that are good, pure, lovely, and praiseworthy.[2] Just let those negative words from ugly people be washed away. Don't dwell on those things.

HEALTHY CONFLICT

There are times in healthy relationships that you will have conflict. Conflict happens. In fact, it's necessary to have healthy relationships. Without conflict, one or both sides aren't being honest. It is said that in every relationship, there are dominant and passive members. One person is the alpha, driving the conversation and the direction of the relationship. It's not wrong or right; it just is. But knowing that you may not be the alpha doesn't mean that your opinion matters less than the alpha's. How, then, do you express yourself? If you tend to be the dominant member of the group, do you make it a priority to hear others' thoughts and feelings? If you are a more passive member of the group, do you assert yourself enough to ensure your voice contributes to the conversation?

Conflict is not always a bad thing. Healthy conflict is necessary to have a healthy organization. It's healthy for you to voice your concerns and disagreements rather than suppress them. When you hide back your feelings and emotions for a while, you suppress your identity. You disable your agency—the control of your life and destiny. God doesn't want you to avoid your emotions. He doesn't want you to suppress your opinions. He does ask you to submit to authority. Some people believe submission is giving up your right to exist. But that isn't God's definition of submission. His call to submission is acknowledging and voluntarily yielding to a higher authority. It is done from a place of humility, mutual respect, and honor—not subjugation.

So, how can you engage in healthy conflict? You need to be aware of the line of authority and when it is the appropriate time to share your comments and feelings. A public setting may not be the best time to disagree with your parents or boss, but the exact time to disagree with your councilman, mayor, or state representative. It depends on the relationship as to what makes the time and place appropriate. I have never understood the phrase at some weddings, "If there is anyone here who does not agree to the joining of these two souls, let him speak now or forever hold his peace." The wedding ceremony is not the time! Although it makes a great climax in a movie, in real life, it shows a huge disrespect to the bride and groom, their parents, and the wedding party itself.

Good conflict helps to bring awareness to problems and then seeks to solve those problems. Healthy conflict brings light to any situation. So, getting along doesn't shy away from conflict, but avoids

WHAT IT MEANS TO GET ALONG

bullies, avoids those that only want to blame others, and tears them down. In a healthy conflict, all parties feel heard and respected. There is a mutual goal toward a solution that benefits everyone. Open communication and strengthened bonds are at the heart of healthy conflict.

Approaching conflict in a healthy manner is a valuable skill to develop. Here is a checklist that will help you with your next conflict:

1. **Avoid personal attacks.** Keep to the issue at hand rather than bringing attacks to someone's character.

2. **Avoid accusations.** Ask questions that start with "what" rather than "why" (we will talk about this later).

3. **Talk about your own experiences rather than labeling others.** I had a theatre teacher who gave pop quizzes rather than scheduled tests, talked about himself all the time, and seemed to find ways to provoke his students. I argued with him in his office saying, "You are so annoying and arrogant!" He responded, "No, you are annoyed at what you perceive as arrogance." That didn't help me calm down then, but I understand now what he meant. I was labeling him instead of expressing my feelings and describing my experience.

4. **Understand the goal of the conflict.** What's the point of your confrontation? Are you trying to resolve an issue or do you just want to be right? Is connection the goal, or do you have another motive? If all parties are trying to find a solution, then the conflict can be resolved. But if there are ulterior motives or hidden agendas, a solution might not be possible today. An argument for the sake of arguing is pointless and will take you further from the goal of resolution.

5. **Have the courage to say what needs to be said.** Keeping the first four points in mind, you can't shy away from expressing yourself during conflict. For the first 20-something years of my marriage, I wouldn't say what I felt. Sometimes I didn't even know what I felt. So, I would give my wife the silent treatment and walk away. But that only led to more frustration. It may be painful to share your feelings at first, but that is often the only way to resolve conflict. Warning: Contents under pressure! You have seen that warning label before. Know that bottling up feelings now will result in a storm later.

UNITY

We have heard from church leaders and the Bible that we should seek unity. But what is unity? Is it conformity of thought? I hope not. Is it an echo chamber of ideas? God, please, no! Does it mean that the leader rules and everyone else just keeps their mouth shut? Again, no. Unity, as referred to in the Bible, means that everyone fulfills their calling and destiny in agreement with the greater mission at hand. Paul said:

> *"Now I plead with you, brethren, by the name of our Lord Jesus Christ, that you all speak the same thing, and that there be no divisions among you, but that you be perfectly joined together in the same mind and in the same judgment."*
>
> 1 Corinthians 1:10, NKJV

The first part says that we should all "speak the same thing." But then it defines this as being "perfectly joined together in the same mind and in the same judgment." This seems to imply that no one can have differing opinions. The following verses, however, describe

WHAT IT MEANS TO GET ALONG

the divisions as being petty allegiances and loyalties to those who preached the gospel to them. Instead of being united under the banner of Christ and who He is, they were building congregations that aligned with who they had heard the gospel from.

Unity in Christ requires us to submit to Jesus and each other.[3] But God gave us minds to think and have opinions so we can further discussion and strengthen one another. If everyone had the same ideas and thoughts, then where would the creativity be? The saying goes, "If you and I are the same, then one of us is irrelevant."

We all bring our unique gifts and thoughts when we come together to accomplish a mission. It's important to make allowances for that difference. That difference should be celebrated. Some people believe that just by putting people of a different color or nationality into the mix you will automatically get diversity of thought. That could not be further from the truth. People of different races often have the same beliefs, and people of different nationalities could also have the same values and tendencies. It is in our personality make-up that we differ. Assumptions based on socioeconomic backgrounds, geographical location, or skin color are not valid.

BUILDING RELATIONSHIPS

Building relationships takes time and effort. The Bible says in Proverbs to have friends you must first be friendly.[4] How do you build relationships? What do you do to invite people into your space? Into your friend group or maybe just into your life? Adding friends on Facebook is easy. Just a few clicks, and you can have hundreds of "friends." But we know that those aren't really friends. Those may not even be acquaintances. You may have a friend of a friend of a

THE **ART** OF **CONNECTION**

friend send you a request, and you just say yes because you seem to have a number of the same friends (and you don't want to be rude).

Making friends in the real world is hard. It takes time and some effort. Yet, most of us would say that the day we met a certain friend, it just seemed to "click." But what had to happen before the proverbial "click?"

More than likely, you decided to go where people were. You may have decided to participate in an activity that others were doing. To say it more directly, you were available to meet other people.

Then, at that event or activity, you decided to interact with those around you. For some, this is harder than for others. I'm mostly introverted. I am perfectly happy going to places and not talking to anyone. However, in some situations, I am forced to act like an extrovert. In those times, I do enjoy meeting new people and sharing life with them. That is a decision I make.

What happens next? Do you go home and never speak to the people you met that day again? Sometimes. But, the day you met your best friend, you made plans to meet again. Maybe you got their cell number or Instagram handle? Man, this seems like a lot of work! True, and it may exhaust the introvert, but if you see the value of having friends, you do it anyway.

Over time, you discover that some of your friends you really connect with, while others, you are happy to let stay on the surface. To engage in deeper, meaningful relationships, you must be vulnerable. This is where things get sticky. Opening your life to new people feels dangerous. It can be. You can get hurt. It's a risk everyone must take in order to have meaningful relationships. But the reward is worth the risk when you find your tribe. When you find a group of people

WHAT IT MEANS TO GET ALONG

and connect with a few individuals who really get you and you get them—the reward is rich.

But still, you need to know how to get along. You need to know what it takes to be "friendly." That's what we will explore in the following chapters.

BEING A PEACEMAKER

Part of getting along is answering God's call to become peacemakers. That is what this book strives to do. A peacemaker is one who seeks out people of peace, and where there is conflict, helps to bring peace. That doesn't require people to compromise their beliefs, though it may ask people to think about things differently. You may need to learn a new skill to be a peacemaker. You may need to change your response to fear, anger, and conflict. If you see conflict as an opportunity for growth, then it isn't as scary to have hard conversations with your boss or employees ... or children ... or spouse.

> IF YOU SEE CONFLICT AS AN OPPORTUNITY FOR GROWTH, THEN IT ISN'T AS SCARY TO HAVE HARD CONVERSATIONS WITH YOUR BOSS OR EMPLOYEES ... OR CHILDREN ... OR SPOUSE.

Jesus said, "Blessed are the peacemakers."[5] And then Paul said, "And let the peace that comes from Christ rule in your hearts. For as members of one body you are called to live in peace. And always be thankful."[6] So clearly, we need to be actively working towards peace in us and around us.

THE ART OF CONNECTION

Letting peace rule in our hearts is a guide to making decisions. We often make choices that we don't feel good about. You have probably had that moment of uneasiness after walking into a room or buying something. You might chalk that up to normal anxiety. But don't write that off. The Holy Spirit works with us in our decision-making by that same peace. Some refer to it as a "check" in their spirit or a feeling in their gut. Whatever you call it, listen to it. God may be warning you of an unwanted result or unpleasant circumstance.

One Saturday afternoon, when my friends and I were riding in the church van toward the lake for swimming, I had one of those moments where my peace abruptly left. I didn't know what would cause it or why that would happen on the way to the lake. I began to pray quietly to myself. My friend noticed, and he said he also had a sudden bad "feeling." One of the girls in the seats behind us asked us what was going on. "Why are you guys praying and looking so concerned?" Neither of us could give an answer. When we finally broke through the brush and into the clearing by the swimming area, the suburban in front of us stopped suddenly. Then, several young men with bats, chains, and other potential weapons got out and started running towards some cars in the parking area.

That's the moment we knew why we had received that warning. My friend put the van in reverse, and we got out of there. We would swim somewhere else that day.

In relationships, this peace monitoring system will guide you in your conversations. You may need just to shut your mouth. Or you may need to ask questions of who you are talking about to gauge their apprehension about the topic or the decision at hand. Don't ignore it. The times I have ignored the peace of God in my spirit, I

WHAT IT MEANS TO GET ALONG

have regretted the results. When Paul told us to let "the peace that comes from Christ rule in our hearts," the word rule there means to act as an umpire. God's peace should have an active role in your decision-making and how you relate to people. If you decide that you want to honor people and see them as God sees them, ask God to help you do this each day. His peace will be that umpire for you. Paul instructed us:

> *"Don't worry about anything; instead, pray about everything. Tell God what you need, and thank Him for all He has done. Then you will experience God's peace, which exceeds anything we can understand. His peace will guard your hearts and minds as you live in Christ Jesus."*
>
> PHILIPPIANS 4:6-7, NLT

To avoid stress and anxiety, we are to pray; to cast our burdens on Jesus and thank Him for what He has done and what He will do. This practice brings the peace that guards our hearts. It acts like a protective barrier against worry. In the context of relationships, we should pray for one another. Pray for each other's needs. Let God's peace be extended, not only to your heart but to the hearts of those around you.

With the combination of daily, unceasing prayer and leaning on God to guide us with His peace, we have an advantage as believers when relating with others. Unfortunately, we don't always use what God has given us. We too easily lose sensitivity to His Spirit and to the peace that He gives us. You can't avoid all conflict, but you can avoid unhealthy conflict—the kind that tears down people and doesn't find solutions, only passes the blame.

THE **ART** OF **CONNECTION**

Now that we know what getting along looks like. How do we accomplish it? Let's go back to the first scripture we read in this chapter, the one that says, "… as much as depends on you."[7] So what depends on you? What can you do about living in peace with others? Let's look at the next chapter and learn how to avoid the poison of criticism.

ENDNOTES

1. See Romans 12:9.
2. See Philippians 4:8.
3. See Ephesians 6.
4. See Proverbs 18:24.
5. Matthew 5:9, NKJV.
6. Colossians 3:15, NLT.
7. Romans 12:18, NKJV.

WHAT IT MEANS TO GET ALONG

CHAPTER TWO
DISCUSSION GUIDE

SUMMARY POINTS

- Getting along doesn't mean being passive—it means taking responsibility for your part in relationships, while recognizing others have free will.

- We should seek out and invest in relationships with "people of peace" (see Luke 10) and set boundaries with those who are toxic or abusive.

- Healthy conflict is necessary for growth and should be approached with respect, honesty, and a goal of resolution.

- Unity in Christ is about shared mission and respect for diversity, not uniformity or forced agreement.

- God's peace acts as an internal compass for relational decisions—prayer and spiritual sensitivity are key to maintaining peace.

THE **ART** OF **CONNECTION**

DISCUSSION QUESTIONS • • • • • • • • • • • • •

1. How can you tell when you're taking too much responsibility in a relationship—or too little?

2. What does it mean to seek out 'people of peace' in your life? How can you recognize them?

3. When have you experienced healthy conflict that led to growth or healing?

4. How does your personality (dominant or passive) influence how you handle conflict?

5. What role does God's peace play in your decision-making, especially in relational tension?

CHAPTER THREE

AVOID THE POISON OF CRITICISM

CRITICISM KILLS RELATIONSHIPS

Criticism kills relationships. I should write that again. ***Criticism kills relationships.*** On my journey towards becoming the best version of me, I became aware of my tendency toward criticism. It is a poison. Constant criticism tells the listener that they are not enough—that they do not and may never measure up. It destroys the strength of emotional bonds until even people who love each other deeply can feel completely disconnected from one another. For those who knew me for the first forty years of my life, I sincerely ask for your forgiveness. I grew up in a critical home and knew nothing different. Both of my parents were fluent in "critical speak." My dad never said the words, "You aren't enough," but he also never said he was proud of me. And in the rare moments he attempted praise, it was always followed by what I could have done to be better.

Criticism increases drama and decreases communication. Years ago, my son, about ten years old, tried to talk to me about a girl. He and I were in my truck, either going to or leaving our

THE ART OF CONNECTION

martial arts school, or it might have been baseball practice. I don't remember what I said, but it was something like, "You're too young for girlfriends," or "We don't date; we hang out with friends." He didn't ask for my advice. He didn't ask any questions, actually. He was just trying to tell me that some girl liked him and what he thought about her. He was attempting to connect with me—share his life. I didn't know it then, but when I responded negatively to him, that is when he decided that he wasn't going to talk to me about anything ... ever again.

My comments, maybe true, maybe not, didn't help him gain the wisdom I tried to share. Instead, I implied, "You're not smart enough or mature enough to have a conversation about girls." I shut him down before he even got a few words out. This behavior exemplifies my complete and total lack of awareness.

At that time in my life, I was an arrogant, self-centered, know-it-all jerk. (In other books, I used stronger language to emphasize this point. No need to repeat that sentiment here.) I actually thought that people *wanted* to hear my opinions of their life, or how they were doing everything wrong.

As an example, a few months after my wife and I were married, she asked me what I wanted for lunch. She was going to make a sandwich for me. I asked for a peanut butter and jelly sandwich—probably my favorite kind of sandwich. After she brought it to me, I told her how she hadn't put enough jelly on it. Also, I instructed her on the proper way to spread the peanut butter. She told me, "Brandon, if you don't like the way I make them, you can do it yourself!" I have been making my own peanut butter and jelly sandwiches now for the last 28 years.

AVOID THE POISON OF CRITICISM

You would think I would have learned after that event. Unfortunately, no. It took several more years for me to understand the breadth and depth of my disease of the mouth. That poison kept dripping from my lips and creating stress and dysfunction in my friendships and my relationship with my wife and children.

Eventually, after several broken relationships and a huge strain on my marriage nearly destroyed me, I humbled myself. I began to see that I was the problem.

I had to change—not them.

All the other chapters in this book assert a positive trait or skill. This one, however, deals with killing bad behavior. Until you deal with stopping the poison coming from within, it will be difficult to turn on the faucet to speak words of life.

> UNTIL YOU DEAL WITH STOPPING THE POISON COMING FROM WITHIN, IT WILL BE DIFFICULT TO TURN ON THE FAUCET TO SPEAK WORDS OF LIFE.

Chances are, self-awareness will only get you halfway there, though. There is a spiritual aspect at the heart of this issue. The root of your critical behavior may come from being a high-achiever and accepting nothing but flawless behavior and results from yourself and others. Maybe you see "almost perfect" as failure and believe that pointing out flaws and imperfections is your responsibility to "help" others become better. Maybe it is a fear of failure that drives you, or remarkably, it might stem from low self-esteem that manifests as perfectionism.

THE ART OF CONNECTION

You, like me, may need inner healing. You may need to ask God to show you where you were hurt in the past. It is possible that some trauma you incurred in your childhood or adolescence began the destructive pattern of behavior of criticism. If that resonates with you, I recommend you read *Think Differently, Live Differently* by Bob Hamp. I have chosen not to focus on the process of inner healing in this book, but understanding what it is and opening yourself up to it can help you become aware of certain limiting or destructive behaviors. Some of these may just be bad habits—learned behaviors from employers, family, or friends. I have good news for you: behavior that has been learned can be unlearned.

So, let's become aware together, starting with the question, "What is criticism?"

WHAT IS CRITICISM?

> **Criticism (n):** 1. *the act of expressing disapproval and of noting the problems or faults of a person or thing; the act of criticizing someone or something.* 2. *a remark or comment that expresses disapproval of someone or something.*[1]

This definition allows for many of our comments, facial expressions, or actions to be considered critical. It is easy to point out faults and communicate our disapproval. Too easy.

Criticism doesn't have to be stated directly; it can be implied. For example, when I suggested to my wife a better way of making a sandwich, I didn't say the words, "You made it wrong," but I certainly criticized the way she had made my sandwich. My disapproval was **implied**. Someone who points out another's faults implies

AVOID THE POISON OF CRITICISM

disapproval of that person or their actions. But that isn't the only way someone can imply disapproval.

You can imply disapproval of your child's behavior by simply leaving the room. Or by not showing up to their sporting event (dance recital, etc.). You can imply disapproval or criticism by your RBF—resting bitter face. (I know that it goes by another name, but this is a Christian book).

My pastor used to tell people that they needed a check-up from the neck-up. That if you are happy and you know it, your face should surely show it. I still have to concentrate on this because my resting face is a frown. And since I usually wear a beard (I haven't seen my actual face in many years), I look rather gruff.

All this to say, that implied criticism is still criticism. You may not even be aware of how your facial expressions or body language are being received. That doesn't change your responsibility to avoid criticism screaming from your face.

Another form of criticism is **comparison**. Comparison matches someone against another person and measures between the two. Sometimes, we do this kind of criticism to ourselves. We compare ourselves to others and find we don't measure up. Other times, our friends or family compare us to others. Either way, we put ourselves on display only to be cut down by our shortcomings. The Apostle Paul said it like this: "For we dare not class ourselves or compare ourselves with those who commend themselves. But they, measuring themselves by themselves and comparing themselves among themselves, are not wise."[2]

Comparison is an internal criticism of others and sometimes of ourselves.

THE ART OF CONNECTION

Stated criticism is more harsh. It used to be, in polite company, that one would not criticize directly or in front of others. But today, behind the safety of social media, people feel free (safe) to say whatever they want about whoever they want when they are online. When I was growing up, I was feeling brave one day and made a comment to another guy on the bus. He punched me in the face. It was a hard lesson, but one that I took to heart. Today, on social media, there are no real consequences for rudeness—not enough people are getting punched in the face to learn those lessons. In fact, some people really enjoy the adrenaline of sparring online, feeding off the negative energy. There is a certain kind of "high" that comes from feeling "better than" others. Being critical makes you feel superior without having to provide any evidence to support that claim.

> TODAY, ON SOCIAL MEDIA, THERE ARE NO REAL CONSEQUENCES FOR RUDENESS—NOT ENOUGH PEOPLE ARE GETTING PUNCHED IN THE FACE TO LEARN THOSE LESSONS.

What isn't included in my definition of criticism? The illusion of passive-aggressive communication. Many people look for reasons to be offended. They try to find some comment, some response that will reinforce their belief that they are a victim. So, they find ways to convey their negativity without directly expressing it. This is called passive-aggressive behavior. They focus on benign behavior and twist it to support a narrative that someone hurt them or has some ulterior motive. Passive aggressiveness shows up as deliberately delaying tasks or responsibilities, intentionally forgetting important things or appointments, sarcasm, giving the

AVOID THE POISON OF CRITICISM

silent treatment, intentionally making mistakes to sabotage things, or making excuses.

Sadly, instead of having their needs met, they usually are neglected because they haven't actually been expressed. Like criticism, it is a relationship killer ... but it is not the topic of this chapter.

RESULTS OF CRITICISM

In this section, we will discuss the many negative ways criticism harms people. We'll talk about what criticism does to the recipient and how criticism kills relationships.

When I was a kid, my dad would ask me and my brother to help with the lawn. Ignoring the fact that I was highly allergic to grass and that the days following such activity sent me into asthmatic fits of snot and coughing, it was a job that young men are often asked to do. But what really made my experience negative wasn't my allergies; it was the impossible, unreachable standard of performance that my dad gave us. He said that he didn't want one stray blade of grass on the sidewalk. To anyone who knows the wind in North Texas, you understand how ludicrous that requirement sounds. Yet, under the fear of beating, we did our best to comply. No matter how hard we tried and how meticulous we were, it was never perfect. Our performance was never enough.

Today, I hire people to do my lawn. Not just because my allergies still don't allow it, but I just don't want anything to do with lawn work. Criticism, coupled with my dad's unrealistic requirements, made me hate the task. This is called avoidance and withdrawal. This can happen in many areas of a person's life. The one that bothers me most happens in church life when the "religious leaders" put

THE ART OF CONNECTION

unrealistic burdens on the people. When leaders are constantly judgmental, it creates a withdrawal from the institution Jesus put in place to reach the world.

Criticism has real consequences. It sucks the life out of people. More directly, it has a lasting impact on the recipient. I contend that there are six results of criticism. They are:

1. defensiveness,
2. self-doubt,
3. avoidance and withdrawal,
4. reduced motivation and support,
5. emotional distress,
6. and relationship strain.

We fostered a young girl years ago who had been taken from the home of a couple of meth addicts. The first night she stayed with us, my wife tried to run a bath for her. At the sight of the bath, this girl started screaming and tried to get away from the water. Apparently, she had been scalded by her stupid parents or guardians. It took some coaxing, but eventually, she learned that we wouldn't do that to her. She began playing with toys and enjoying bath time like most kids do (it took some time). Her initial response was **defensiveness**. She reacted to the sight of the running water even before she felt that it wasn't going to scald her. Part of her response was **avoidance and withdrawal**, trying to get out of the bathroom. But her initial reaction was to try and protect herself from the water and let everyone know she wasn't happy about it.

AVOID THE POISON OF CRITICISM

That's defensiveness. You immediately let everyone know why you're right and everyone else is wrong. It is emotional Taekwondo! "You have something to say to me? I've got a block and an attack! Ha!" This response to criticism is aggressive insecurity—**emotional distress**. Everyone around you knows when it's happening, but no one may say anything to you for fear of the emotional Taekwondo.

Another result of criticism is **self-doubt.** The constant barrage of critical words as arrows thrown at you can make you question every decision you make. By the time I was fourteen, I realized that I had not made a decision on my own. I had only followed. I followed my parents or my brother in every choice I made until then. That's when I decided to leave my mother's house and live with my father. That began a series of bad decisions on my part. There were some good ones thrown in every once in a while. But for the most part, they weren't beneficial. I can tell you that I had tons of self-doubt. Those bad decisions were met not only with the consequences of making bad decisions but also with a heap of criticism from my dad, brother, and my mother. This **reduced** all my **motivation** and removed any **support**. The constant barrage of criticism created a **relational strain** with every person I was connected to—family, friends, and coworkers alike.

In what areas do you most struggle to make a decision? Has someone at some time bombarded you with criticism? You may have one or more of these six results at work in your life: defensiveness, self-doubt, avoidance and withdrawal, reduced motivation and support, emotional distress, and a strain on your relationships. Do you repeat the pattern of criticism toward others?

Take a personal inventory. Become self-aware. If you have some soul work to do to find healing and freedom, then do it. Your life will get immensely better, and your relationships will all benefit from removing the wounds of criticism from your past and erasing the behavior of criticism from your future.

THE MYTH OF CONSTRUCTIVE CRITICISM

We have all heard the term "constructive criticism." It is supposed to be a welcome version of criticism for the receiver. I have not found that to be true. Most of the time, it is just criticism. Poisonous and destructive. But since people believe it to be a good thing, let's look at how it is delivered and what can make it just as negative.

First, people believe that if they have a relationship with someone strong enough to withstand "honest conversations," then everything will work out. Listen, only a relationship grounded in love and from a deep place of trust that you have each other's highest and best interest at heart can survive a round of constructive criticism. If you don't have that kind of relationship, you should definitely not engage. Even when you do, know that the criticism can *still* leave bruises that will need healing later. My question is this: if you love someone and have a strong relationship with them, why not encourage them instead? Reinforcing good behavior creates a more positive result than criticizing poor behavior.

Other examples are when employers, teachers, or other leaders believe that their position gives them the authority to "speak into" a situation. There are cases where an employer or a spiritual authority, like your pastor, needs to have a hard conversation. But the emphasis here is an adjustment—course correction. It is not a general identification of a fault, but a "Hey, stop this, or something very bad will happen!" It's more of a rescue scenario rather than helping you become a better employee or a better follower of Jesus.

AVOID THE POISON OF CRITICISM

Constructive criticism is an oxymoron. It's a myth. Most of the time it leads to the same negative results we discussed in the previous section.

CHANGING THE HABIT OF CRITICISM

Most of the time, you should keep criticism to yourself. When you notice an area that could use improvement, instead of criticizing the person, perhaps you should employ a coaching approach. I'm not talking about a football head coach who screams at you until you get it right approach. Rather, ask compelling, curious questions that help the person receive greater awareness of the issue. This awareness comes from within. It is an "A-ha!" for the person who is now exploring the situation that just happened by answering a series of questions that cause them to look at it from an outside perspective.

We will talk more about asking curious, probing questions later. They are a powerful tool for learning to get along with people. For now, let's think about what alternatives to criticism you might engage in to help those around you properly. How can you avoid criticism while helping others become the best version of themselves?

First, recognize that it isn't your responsibility to help people change. Unless they ask you to become their life coach—it ain't your job! Yes, we want what's best for people. Clearly, their rage towards others isn't what is best. Or, the way they do a project may not be the best way, but that's not for you to point out. You may ask them questions. Ask, "What motivated you to do it that way?" or "What are some other ways you may have done this?" These questions get them to think about their actions without accusation or criticism.

THE ART OF CONNECTION

A coaching method requires you to be curious about people. It necessitates that you see them as smart, capable human beings. A coaching perspective doesn't automatically assume that you know the best answer. You may get into your questions and discover that the person you thought was doing it wrong was actually doing it better.

When you are tempted to criticize, think about the long-term impact. Sure, you might force someone to make a temporary behavioral change, but at what cost? And will they develop the skills and insights to grow or will they just lose confidence in themselves and their abilities and potentially put up defenses with you? If you genuinely care about people and you want to walk with them for the long haul, reframe criticism through the lens of encouragement.

Ask yourself these questions:

- How can I improve in this area?
- In what ways can I incorporate this into my life?
- What barriers do I face that keep me from adding this behavior to my life?

Learn how to coach yourself through this book and through this process. The better coach you become to yourself, the better coach you will be to others.

ENDNOTES

1. https://www.britannica.com/dictionary/criticism.
2. 2 Corinthians 10:12, NKJV.

AVOID THE POISON OF CRITICISM

CHAPTER THREE
DISCUSSION GUIDE

SUMMARY POINTS

- Criticism—whether spoken, implied, or through comparison—erodes trust, emotional safety, and relationship health.

- Root causes of criticism often include trauma, perfectionism, and low self-worth, and healing requires intentional reflection and spiritual awareness.

- Criticism results in defensiveness, self-doubt, avoidance, emotional distress, and damaged relationships.

- Constructive criticism is often just criticism in disguise and can still harm unless grounded in deep relational trust.

- A coaching approach—asking questions with curiosity instead of judgment—can inspire growth and maintain a vibrant relational connection.

THE **ART** OF **CONNECTION**

DISCUSSION QUESTIONS • • • • • • • • • • • •

1. How have you experienced the negative effects of criticism—either as a giver or receiver?

2. What early life experiences may have shaped your critical tendencies or sensitivity to criticism?

3. Can you think of a time when criticism damaged a relationship you cared about? How might you approach it differently now?

4. How could adopting a coaching mindset—asking questions instead of criticizing—change your closest relationships?

5. In what ways do you still struggle with implied criticism (tone, facial expression, silence), and how can you begin to shift?

CHAPTER FOUR

PRAISE FREELY

> *"A person needs praise like a plant needs water."*
>
> RUDOLF DREIKURS

WHAT IS PRAISE?

Praise means to commend or applaud personal worth or actions, to give honor to; in short, praise is encouragement. When we freely praise those around us each day, we choose to embolden them—build them up. We remind them that God has gifted them and called them to their purpose. When we praise them, we reinforce their faith in God and their faith in themselves. When I discuss praising freely, what I am encouraging you to do is create several tiny moments of encouragement throughout your day.

God told Joshua, "Be strong and of good courage."[1] What does that mean? Well, to encourage means to pour courage in—you give them some of yours. At the time God gave these words to Joshua, he was about 80 years old, and he had been the executive assistant for Moses for the last 40 years. Moses had led a bunch of fickle, complaining people through the wilderness. Scholars believe that the journey shouldn't have taken more than 11 or 12 days—a month with a margin for things to go wrong and to wrangle that many people, animals, and belongings. It certainly shouldn't have taken more than a few years after their exodus from Egypt. We know the story; however, the extended version took forty years, and it was a time of trial for the Israelites. Mostly, it was a leadership development course for Moses, Joshua, and the elders of the people.

But then, after that 40-year training course, the people were finally ready to enter the promised land. But wait, Moses couldn't go in. He died just before the people crossed the Jordan into the next phase of their history. In these short verses at the opening of the book of Joshua, God tells him to be strong and of good courage three times. Why?

Because he needed it.

The tasks behind had been monumental. The tasks ahead looked impossible. Nevertheless, Joshua headed in feet first.

Why is it important for you and the people around you to have courage? We live in a world where fear and doubt and evil run rampant. We are fixated on mental health, depression, anxiety, and trauma triggers. When you meet people in the grocery store, a coffee shop, or at your office, you can bet that they are going through some kind of storm.

A pastor I know once said that everyone is either going through a storm, entering a storm, or just got out of a storm. Life is full of storms. They happen. Sometimes, they happen because of our own actions, sometimes because of someone else's actions, and sometimes for no recognizable reason other than "just because." So we need to

PRAISE FREELY

be ready for them. We need courage. Courage sees, courage speaks, and courage acts.

COURAGE SEES

Courage sees by looking forward by the leading of the Holy Spirit. You have heard it said that hope isn't a strategy. You won't be motivated by merely hope. You need clear goals and a path to get where you want to go. Yesterday, I spoke to some small business entrepreneurs. It was a last-minute engagement, but I decided to take the group through a strategic planning session. First, we talked about where they were now in their business. Sometimes, locating yourself and identifying your metrics, both financial and non-financial, can be difficult. You have to be honest with yourself and the numbers. Once we had the businesses located on their "now" section of the page, we then began to look at where they wanted to go.

Instead of making vague descriptions of growth or success, I asked them to bring some clarity to their vision. If they want to grow sales, by how much? If they wanted to increase their staff, by how many? If they wanted to improve their branding and marketing message, how would they quantify success?

I asked them these questions because when you have a clear vision of where you want to go, you can then plan how you will get there. The vision comes first; then, you can muster the courage to take the next steps. Jesus was able to endure the pain of the cross because of vision—the joy that was set before Him—because He saw you and me reconciled to the Father.[2] It was because of what He **saw** that He could endure the cross. Courage **sees** what is possible with God and believes that with Him, you can do all things.[3] Courage sees the barriers but believes that with God, you can overcome them.

THE ART OF CONNECTION

COURAGE SPEAKS

Courage speaks. Courage says what it will do; it declares the will of God boldly and aligns its conversations toward the goals. In 1996, my church sent a delegation to the Olympics in Atlanta, Georgia. We had a team of about seven people traveling fourteen hours in a van across the lower states from Central Texas. Two people were not from our church but had been excited to go to the Olympics, not to watch the events, but to witness to those who visited from all over the world.

> COURAGE SAYS WHAT IT WILL DO; IT DECLARES THE WILL OF GOD BOLDLY AND ALIGNS ITS CONVERSATIONS TOWARDS THE GOALS.

Along the way, one of the guys from the other church had a habit of negative speech. He talked about how the van might break down, how we might not find a place to eat, or how we might get in an accident miles away from home. Every time he opened his mouth, he had to make a derogatory comment about something. About two-thirds of the way through the trip, I had had enough. At the time, I was only twenty-two years old, and I had been married only a few months. I wasn't very experienced in life, but I knew that our team couldn't take much more of the negativity. This guy was probably twice my age, but I didn't let it stop me from telling him to shut up! I admonished him to stop with all the curses over our journey. After that, he stayed quiet. Thankfully another member of the team who was his age backed me up. She was tired of hearing it as well.

The Apostle Paul said, "Since we have the same spirit of faith, according to what is written, **'I believed and therefore I spoke,'** we

PRAISE FREELY

also believe and therefore we speak."⁴ Words matter. God used His words to form and create the world. We use our words to create the world we live in. We need to use our words to shape our thoughts and encourage ourselves towards the good works that God has called us to do. We can also use our words to build others up or tear them down. Courage speaks blessing. Courage speaks what God says about yourself and others around you.

COURAGE ACTS

Courage acts. Courage takes the steps needed to see the will of God accomplished. Let's go back to what God said to Joshua: "Only be strong and very courageous, that you may observe to do according to all the law which Moses my servant commanded you; do not turn from it to the right hand or to the left, that you may prosper wherever you go."⁵ Courage does something about what it sees and what it speaks. It's not enough to be a hearer only, but a doer of the Word.

> *"But be **doers** of the Word, and not hearers only, deceiving yourselves."*
>
> JAMES 1:22, NKJV (EMPHASIS ADDED)

We can't be people who draw back. We cannot be people who see the challenge laid out before us and then choose to do nothing. Paul instructed the Hebrews, "But we are not of those who *draw back* to perdition, but of those who believe to the saving of the soul."⁶ Courage accepts the challenge. It decides that the pain of staying is more than the pain of taking up the challenge ahead.

Now that you know more about how courage acts, how do you pour that into those around you? Remember, to encourage means to pour courage in.

THE ART OF CONNECTION

One way is by having "ICNU" conversations. That's an "I see in you" conversation. Remember that courage sees. When you tell someone that you see leadership in them, that you see good character in them, it builds them up. I had a staff accountant who wasn't producing well. I scheduled a meeting to discuss our expectations and how he could improve. During the meeting, I got the impression that he just needed some encouragement. I knew that he had been raised by a single mom and hadn't had much affirmation from his dad. So, I had an ICNU conversation. I told him that I saw him as a very talented accountant and that I knew he was capable of much more. I told him that one day, he would either have his own firm or he would manage the entire tax department of a large firm. All of which was true. He was smart and very capable. From that day forward, he began to act like the person I described. He started to believe that he was that person.

I poured courage into him. That courage enlarged him.

My mother used to say, "If you don't have anything nice to say, don't say anything at all." It's good advice. To encourage someone means that you speak good things about people. Not only should you refrain from negative comments, but if you think of a kind word for someone, don't hold on to it—speak it!

I was driving by another accounting firm one day and saw one of my former employees getting into their car. I thought of several of their strengths and how I thought they would do so well at their new job. When I got to where I was going, I sent them a text to tell them so. So many times, we have these positive thoughts towards others, employees, friends, or family, and we just hold it in. Let it out! Why are we so quick to share negative comments on social media or in

PRAISE FREELY

groups in person, but we don't share comments that build each other up? Let's change that dynamic.

Part of praising freely includes stirring up others to do good works. **Courage acts.** So to encourage we point people towards making good decisions, towards fulfilling their responsibilities, towards reaching their goals.

> "And let us consider one another in order to stir up love and good works."
>
> HEBREWS 10:24, NKJV

Pastors encourage as part of their main responsibility. But so do parents and teachers, supervisors and managers. Anyone who influences others should see it as their responsibility to point people towards fulfilling all that God has called them to. Some teachers get into their careers because they love or have a talent for the subject matter. Math teachers who love math, art teachers who love art, etc. But that love then translates to a desire to pass on what they know. There are only a few teachers who really understand the next level— that they have an opportunity to influence and encourage someone. Those teachers see past the homework and the tests and see the potential residing in the bodies sitting in their class.

My art teacher in high school was that kind of teacher. He wasn't a big guy. At five foot eight inches and maybe 170 pounds, he didn't stand out in a crowd. Yet, to me, he was a big man. He was firm but fair in managing his class. He encouraged me when no one else did. I'm sure I did many things that he didn't like, but he never acted like he didn't like me as a person. He saw value in every student. I am one of many students who were impacted by his fathering style of teaching.

THE ART OF CONNECTION

Pouring courage into people changes their lives. It causes them to reach for their goals and dreams. It helps them see their potential and helps them get out of their own way. Putting into practice daily encouragement builds up the people around you. With it, you invest in them. You make deposits of hope and life that will produce a harvest if watered with more encouragement. Encouragement doesn't depend on others doing what you want or saying nice things to you. It depends on the choice you make.

HOW TO ENCOURAGE

We talked about what it means to encourage, that you are pouring in courage. Now, let's focus on the practical application—beginning to encourage others in your daily life. For those of us for whom that doesn't happen naturally, we need to be intentional. But for those just starting out, being intentional (doing it on purpose) may not sound very sincere. Or, you may *overdo* it, which also may not sound sincere. I'll use praise and encouragement interchangeably here.

The word praise is often used as a part of the worship of God. And yes we are to spend a good amount of effort in praise to our God. Praise is telling God (and others) about all the good things He has done and about all the good that He is. Encouraging or praising others is very similar. It focuses on their nature and their actions.

When someone does something well, tell them. The emphasis here should be on the effort more than the results. In Carol Dusek's book *Mindset*, she discusses how those who are praised early in life for their results often develop a fixed mindset. A fixed mindset is one that doesn't believe that it can grow or learn new things. Once they receive praise for certain results, they are less likely to engage

PRAISE FREELY

in more challenging activities since they may not produce positive results and, subsequently, positive praise.

In our praise or encouragement of others, we should be conscious to develop a growth mindset in the hearers. One where challenging tasks are accepted with enthusiasm and the hope of learning something new. Direct your praise to the *effort* involved, the hard work and time engaged. Ask what they learned and praise the insight discovered. Your praise in this manner will help develop the growth mindset that helps them believe they can accomplish even greater tasks.

My oldest son was sometimes asked to pitch on one of his little league teams. In one game where he pitched, each batter hit a ground ball to one of the infielders. And because of errors in fielding or throwing, each batter reached base. Once the bases were loaded the coach pulled him. Of course, I was furious with the coach, but I held it in (that day). I went over to my son in the dugout and told him he did a great job. He looked at me like I was insane. I said, "You don't have to throw strikeouts to be a great pitcher. You threw pitches that resulted in easy ground balls that should have resulted in easy outs. All except one of those runners reached base on errors. You did what your team needed." I'm not sure he totally understood that or took it to heart then, but he knew I was proud of him and not disappointed in his endeavor. The point was that great effort doesn't always get the results you want—especially in team sports. Not that you should ever diminish the effort put in by your teammates, but it takes everyone on a team producing great effort for the results you want.

> **GREAT EFFORT DOESN'T ALWAYS GET THE RESULTS YOU WANT.**

THE ART OF CONNECTION

Also, your effort may be at your highest level, but the other team's effort and skills may supersede yours. Does that mean you didn't do well? No. It just means the other team did a bit better.

LET IT OUT

There are many ways to deliver a message of encouragement. Of course, the first and easiest delivery method is your voice. When you see praiseworthy effort, speak up. Many times, we go about our day and keep our praise to ourselves. We may see our kids do something awesome and yet only verbalize what they could have done better. That's not praise, that's criticism. We already discussed how destructive that can be.

Instead of keeping your praise to yourself, let it out. Let those around you hear and know that they are doing well. I still struggle in this area. It's something that I continue to work on. I get pretty intense and driven. That intensity results in tunnel vision sometimes. That's when I don't see the efforts of those around me because I'm so focused on the task ahead. When I split my financial services company with my CPA firm to take on partners at the CPA firm, I told them I was keeping my assistant Maggie on the financial services staff. She had worked for me for a few years by that time. She was surprised. She said, "I didn't even know you liked me as your assistant." That saddened me. I hadn't expressed my appreciation to someone I relied on every day and thought very highly of. My problem was not expressing praise for what she was doing. We will talk about expressing appreciation for others in a later chapter because showing your appreciation is also extremely important. Where praise and encouragement pour courage into the person, appreciation expresses love for the person.

PRAISE FREELY

Other delivery methods for praise and encouragement are handwritten letters, texts, telephone calls, voicemail messages, and, if you must, social media posts. Each can be very effective in verbalizing encouragement. Of course, each can be totally screwed up if not handled properly.

Let's start with handwritten letters or notes. Letters aren't something our society does much of anymore. With email, texts, and other more immediate forms of communication, using snail mail (U.S. Postal Service) just isn't as practical. And that's what makes a handwritten letter that much more special today. That you wrote out your thoughts as legibly as your handwriting will allow, you folded it, and placed it in an envelope with a stamp, shows the amount of time invested in this message.

I used to have a pen pal in high school. I met her at a Baptist youth camp. We weren't romantically involved, both having a girlfriend or boyfriend at the time. But we got along well and got each other's humor. We exchanged addresses and would write every other month or so. That sounds so cheesy and odd now. But there's just something about opening the mailbox and pulling out a hand-addressed letter that has a few pages. You, as the reader, feel special.

Handwritten letters or cards stand out. How long do you save an email? Chances are that handwritten letter will get tucked somewhere and be brought out again when a fresh dose of encouragement is needed.

When I was having a hard day, or I remembered something funny my friend had written, I would go back to the letter and read it again. Handwritten letters of encouragement have a huge impact on the person who received them. Just as Paul wrote so many letters to the early church for their encouragement, you can write a letter, note, or

THE **ART** OF **CONNECTION**

postcard to someone who needs a bit of encouragement. Besides, the post office could really use your business.

Texting created the easiest and most effective delivery method for encouragement. Whatever time of day, or wherever you are, except while driving, when you think of an encouraging word for someone, either by voice to text or voice text, you can send that message of courage right to that person. It doesn't cost anything. Other than the occasional auto-correct error, the message can be clearly understood by the receiver (no handwriting cipher needed). What an amazing tool! But what do we usually use it for? Criticism, gossip, complaining, or just to set up a meeting. Of course, other uses of texting are inappropriate for this book to discuss, so we will focus on the positive uses here.

I often think of things I'd like to say to people to encourage them, but then make the excuse that I didn't get to see them that day. With texting, that really isn't a great excuse anymore. Not that you should send every encouraging thought through your phone to your friends and co-workers. Too much of a good thing becomes an annoyance. There are those among us who are over-texters. You know who you are! You write books from your phone and don't realize that sometimes the thumbs-up emoji means that I'm done with this conversation for now.

Don't be an over-texter! But that isn't most of our problem, is it? Instead, we withhold the encouragement that someone may desperately need. You may be hearing God's voice when someone comes to mind and you send them an encouraging word or scripture. Again, I work on this for myself. The Bible says, "Do not withhold good from whom it is due, when it is in the power of your hands to do so."[7] Sometimes, the good we withhold is encouragement.

PRAISE FREELY

Because of social media, the way we communicate and interact with each other has changed. Many people believe that if they like a post or comment on a post, then they have had some kind of interaction with that person. But that isn't real. It's a form of virtual reality. It is a place where people post the highlights of their lives and sometimes share their dirty laundry with the world. Meanness and rude behavior hide behind the cloak of anonymity. It amazes me what people will say on social media. I once mouthed off to an eighth grader when I was a sixth grader. I received immediate feedback. A punch to my face. Because of the lack of the threat of that kind of immediate feedback, people say the worst kind of things to each other.

But there are those who use social media as a platform for good. They compliment and encourage on a daily basis. However, sometimes I wonder if they are doing it to encourage someone or draw attention to themselves for saying something nice. For example, when a husband tells his wife he loves her on a Facebook post. Can he not just text her himself? Why put that on a public forum such as social media? I'm not saying people shouldn't express themselves on social media. But my concern is that the comments aren't made with pure motives. They are made knowing someone is watching. What you say and do when nobody is watching is a truer test of character. Nevertheless, social media can be a great way to express encouragement to staff and friends publicly. When you want your world, your sphere of influence, to join you in recognizing the great efforts and accomplishments of those you care about, saying it publicly is a good way to do that.

> **WHAT YOU SAY AND DO WHEN NOBODY IS WATCHING IS A TRUER TEST OF CHARACTER.**

THE ART OF CONNECTION

Keeping in mind that social media is a public forum, you should probably not discuss intimate topics there. As a delivery method for praise and encouragement, depending on who the audience is, it can be a powerful tool to pour courage into others.

A WORD ON WHEN

Now, for those of us who don't naturally think about praise and encouragement, I want to offer a few tips on *when* to deliver these powerful messages.

First, I highly recommend following the leading of the Holy Spirit. When God leads you to drop a text to someone or call them, don't hesitate. Solomon said, "A word in due season, how good it is!"[8] That leading may be just the word someone needs at that time. It may seem foolish to you at the time or unimportant, but you don't always know what people are going through. Let God use you to brighten someone's day. Pour courage into their trial. Let God lead you.

After the leading of the Holy Spirit, the next best way to get into a practice of encouragement requires that you schedule times to share praise and encouragement. It may seem forced or cumbersome the first few times you do it, but you will get over the awkwardness. Craig Groeschel began to hand out gold stars on Fridays at the end of the day. He decided to schedule time to tell people they were doing a great job. One day, after he had gone through the office handing them out, a person who had been in the restroom when all the gold stars were being given met him at his car and asked if he should get one too! His staff loved it and now it's a regular thing he schedules into his week.

Another time to appropriately encourage people happens at life events. Changes in jobs, when they get married, when they graduate,

PRAISE FREELY

when they have kids, when a loved one dies. All these life events and more merit the encouraging word. Change brings stress. Even good stress is still stress. An encouraging word during a time of upheaval and change mitigates that stress.

- What will you do today to pour courage into someone else?

- What will you do this week to begin freely praising others an intentional part of your daily life?

In the next chapter, we will discuss what happens when people let you down, when offenses come, or when someone hurts you.

ENDNOTES

1. See Joshua 1:9, NKJV.
2. See Hebrews 12:1-2.
3. See Matthew 19:26.
4. 2 Corinthians 4:13, NKJV (emphasis added).
5. Joshua 1:7, NKJV.
6. Hebrews 10:39, NKJV.
7. Proverbs 3:27, NKJV.
8. Proverbs 15:23, NKJV.

The Art of Connection

Praise and encouragement help people:

- Believe in themselves,
- Manage stress,
- Have confidence and courage to take on obstacles,
- See what is possible,
- Speak confidently about what they want,
- Find the courage take action to see their goals become reality.

PRAISE FREELY

CHAPTER FOUR DISCUSSION GUIDE

SUMMARY POINTS • • • • • • • • • • • • •

- Praise is a form of encouragement that pours courage into others by affirming their character, efforts, and potential.

- True encouragement helps others see their future with hope, speak words of life, and take action despite fear.

- Focusing on effort rather than outcomes promotes a growth mindset and builds lasting motivation.

- Praise can be delivered in many forms—spoken, written, texted, or shared publicly—but it must be sincere and timely.

- Developing a habit of encouragement includes following Holy Spirit nudges, planning moments of praise, and speaking life during stressful transitions.

THE ART OF CONNECTION

DISCUSSION QUESTIONS • • • • • • • • • • •

1. Who poured courage into you during a time of doubt, and how did it impact your actions?

2. What keeps you from giving more encouragement—busyness, awkwardness, forgetfulness?

3. How can you be more intentional about praising effort instead of just outcomes?

4. What practical ways can you deliver more encouragement this week (text, voice, handwritten note, social media)?

5. In what areas of your life do you need to receive more praise—and how can you ask for what you need with vulnerability?

CHAPTER FIVE

EXPRESS APPRECIATION DAILY

I once asked a classroom of students if they could define gratitude without using the words thankful, appreciate, gratefulness, or any of their derivatives or synonyms. Many attempted. All failed to define it without using those words or their synonyms. Even the dictionary uses the synonyms to define the word. I'm sure you're thinking, "I bet I could do it," so go ahead, take a few minutes …

What did you come up with?

Okay, how about the word appreciation? Chances are, words like gratitude, gratefulness, and thankfulness spring to mind.

Now, do you see how difficult it actually is to define appreciation?

If you're a word geek, maybe you went to *Websters 1828 Dictionary* and discovered a timeless definition for appreciation: 1.) A setting a value on; a just evaluation or estimate of merit, weight, or any moral consideration; and 2). A rise in value; an increase of worth or value.

THE ART OF CONNECTION

But since I'm the one writing this book, I'll give you my definition. For me, appreciation has two parts.

1. You must first acknowledge that someone has done something for you or given you something. (This tracks with "a just evaluation of merit" and "setting a value on" it.)

2. You must *express* the appropriate praise, honor, or recognition of what the other person has done. (Stay with me—when you express someone's worth to you, their feelings of significance increase. Like a good investment, they appreciate—"rise in value.")

In the Bible, God commands us, "… **in everything give thanks**; for this is the will of God in Christ Jesus for you."[1] That seems like a no-brainer. We easily understand that we are meant to be thankful to God because every good and perfect gift comes from Him.[2] But expressing appreciation is not meant to stop there. Paul sent a letter to his friends living in Corinth and told them this:

> *"Every time I think of you—and I think of you often!—I thank God for your lives …"*
>
> 1 CORINTHIANS 1:4, MSG

Yes, Paul was thanking God, but he was telling *them* He was thanking God for them. He expressed His appreciation to them. In his letter to the believers in Rome, Paul instructed:

> *"Try to outdo yourselves in respect and honor of one another."*
>
> ROMANS 12:10, TPT

EXPRESS APPRECIATION DAILY

Jesus Himself said:

> *"If I then, your Lord and Teacher, have washed your feet, you also ought to wash one another's feet."*
>
> JOHN 13:14, ESV

This doesn't mean we are supposed to get out a bowl and take off someone's shoes and socks. This passage is a metaphor for how we are to approach others with humility and show them—express to them—honor, respect ... appreciation.

In 2 Timothy 3:2, Paul lists things people will do in the last days. On that list is being unthankful—the opposite of showing appreciation and gratitude.

So, appreciation is biblical, and it requires both acknowledgment and expression. You can have acknowledgment, but if it is not appropriately expressed, how does the person who is the object of your acknowledgment know you appreciate them? It's the *expression* of appreciation that completes the act. Now, how you express appreciation depends on how you give and receive appreciation or love.

In his book, *The 5 Love Languages: The Secret to Love that Lasts*, Dr. Gary Chapman describes five ways that people most often give and receive love. He also describes how important it is to know *how* to convey love in a way that others will "understand" and receive it. Think of it like this: If you only speak Spanish, but I keep talking to you in French, you won't know what I mean, even if every word I say is kind. If I really want to communicate my love for you, I need to learn how to speak in a language you comprehend.

THE ART OF CONNECTION

Later, Chapman partnered with Paul White, Ph.D., and together they wrote *The 5 Languages of Appreciation in the Workplace: Empowering Organizations by Encouraging People*. This book took the concept beyond the realm of family and friends to apply the benefits to your professional life. I highly recommend these two foundational books because they help us understand each other. Understanding is a vital key to getting along.

The five appreciation languages are words of affirmation, acts of service, quality time, tangible gifts, and appropriate physical touch. Suppose someone's appreciation language is tangible gifts, yet you like to show your appreciation by words of affirmation. In that case, even though you are expressing your appreciation the way you know how, they may not feel appreciated by you. I love that Chapman called them languages because appreciation must be communicated, and it sure helps when both parties of the communication interaction speak the same language.

I had a tough time speaking my wife's love language for a long time. I kept trying to tell her how much I loved her by providing things, when her love language is quality time. Until I understood how to show her love, to her, I was wasting money or working too much.

In the workplace, you may have to experiment with how the people around you understand or receive appreciation. If you lead a team, you can have them take The 5 Appreciation Languages test to find out faster.[3] I asked my team to go through the test, and if they wanted, I invited them to share the results with me. A handful of people followed through. For the others, I chose to use multiple methods of appreciation. If someone did an excellent job on a project, I might write them an encouraging email, send them a small gift, and bring

EXPRESS APPRECIATION DAILY

it up in a staff meeting to share with others what they accomplished. I may also take them to lunch with me and my wife.

As a leader, you may also choose to jump in on a project or help clean up after an event to serve your staff. Whatever "washing one another's feet" looks like to you—do that.

One area where you need to be careful is with people whose appreciation language is appropriate physical touch. With remote employees and, let's be real, potential sexual harassment accusations, you probably should limit your touch to a handshake and a pat on the shoulder. Thankfully, most people have more than one appreciation language that they respond to. So even if physical touch is at the top of their list, you may be safer to show your appreciation with the other four.

MENTAL AND PHYSICAL BENEFITS OF GRATITUDE

Studies have shown that an attitude of gratitude can have positive physiological effects. Some of those positive effects that lead to an overall state of well-being are improved heart health, enhanced immune function, better sleep quality, reduced stress levels, pain reduction, improved mental health, enhanced physical health, and longevity.

That's a pretty good list. Let's discuss a few of those.

REDUCED STRESS—

It has been said that it is impossible to be thankful and stressed at the same time. Have you ever taken a thankfulness walk? Try walking around your neighborhood each night, or maybe during the day, walk around your office while counting your blessings.

THE ART OF CONNECTION

When I owned the CPA firm, we had an office in Cedar Park, Texas. That's just north of Austin. Occasionally, when it wasn't too hot, I would go for a walk. Our office was in a business office complex with several businesses per building. There were four or five buildings in this complex, and to walk around the whole thing was about a mile.

My stress levels at the time were high, and these walks helped me get some air and think about all the good things in my life. Sometimes, it was harder than others to think of the good things. Of course, I would start with my beautiful wife. Then my children. And so on ...

SLEEP QUALITY—

Like many of you, I have struggled with getting quality sleep. When I was younger, I could run on just a few hours of sleep and it did not affect my performance during the day. Sometimes, I'd stay up watching movies or reading, or our friends would come over, and we would spend the evening visiting into the early morning. Lack of quality sleep because of poor discipline isn't what we are talking about here. You have to make time for sleep. Your body needs the time to regenerate.

> YOU HAVE TO MAKE TIME FOR SLEEP. YOUR BODY NEEDS THE TIME TO REGENERATE.

What usually keeps me from quality sleep? Thinking about all the things that I did that day or what I will have to do tomorrow. To combat my mind racing through what could possibly go wrong or just rehearsing earlier conversations, I started journaling. Just before bed, I'll get out my iPad and write down my thoughts. I

EXPRESS APPRECIATION DAILY

start by thanking God for what He's doing in and through me. I thank Him for my family. I try to find something that happened that day to be thankful for. Other than having to get up two times to go to the bathroom because I'm over forty, that usually helps me sleep well. A 2009 study published in the *Journal of Psychosomatic Research 66* found that grateful people are less likely to think negative and worrying thoughts and more likely to think positive thoughts. Both of which correlated to better quality of sleep and longer sleep durations.[4]

IMPROVED MENTAL HEALTH—

If you have ever seen the movie *Legally Blonde* with Reese Witherspoon, you may remember the line, "Happy people don't kill their husbands!" While I can't say for sure if the movie can be cited as a source for psychological studies, I can say that there is some truth to it. A study on the role of positive reframing and positive emotion published by *Psychology Press* stated that gratitude decreased (or prevented the increase) in reports of depressive symptoms. They also found that gratitude prompts people to re-frame otherwise negative experiences as potentially positive experiences. This reframing, in turn, related to fewer depressive symptoms.[5]

I already shared how I was fired from my first job as an accountant after I graduated college. It was a traumatic experience for me. It happened right before Christmas on December 22, 2000. I will never forget that day. At the time, I felt lost. I felt like a failure. This wasn't the first time I had been let go from a job, but it was the first time I was fired. Looking back, I know that I caused the firing by my behavior. My arrogance and pride wouldn't let me take orders from a simple bookkeeper.

THE ART OF CONNECTION

Looking back on it now, I am grateful for the experience. I needed to be let go from that job so that I could meet another CPA who would later look to sell his practice. And because I had been fired, I was desperate for work and took a contract job doing bookkeeping for him to help feed my family. Gratitude helped me reframe that incident as a positive event that led to me ultimately purchasing my first CPA firm at thirty-one years old in 2004.

In addition to reframing, gratitude helps to reduce depressive symptoms or thoughts. Depression can be defined as the inability to have positive mental thoughts or attitudes. Being grateful pushes back on depression. When you count your blessings, you make yourself see how good things are in your life. Whatever you are going through, there is always something or someone to be grateful for.

What does that mean for us? Well, to be a person who gets along with anyone, anywhere, you need to be in an overall state of well-being. You need your stress levels to be reduced. You need to have better sleep. You need to be mentally healthy.

SPIRITUAL BENEFITS OF GRATITUDE

According to the Bible, there are several spiritual benefits of gratitude. A quick search will bring up countless times the word thankful or thanksgiving can be found in the Bible.

GRATITUDE ENCOURAGES FELLOWSHIP—

In Luke, Jesus was approached (from a distance) by ten lepers. They followed the law by standing a far distance away. They weren't permitted to be close to anyone except others who were also stricken with the disease. Leprosy makes relationships difficult.

EXPRESS APPRECIATION DAILY

After Jesus healed them, he instructed them to go show themselves to the priest to confirm that they were healed. Only one went back to show his gratitude for the miracle. Because he had been healed, this time, he approached Jesus closely and fell at His feet to worship Him and thank him. Gratitude brought him closer to Jesus.[6]

GRATITUDE ENABLES THE PEACE OF GOD—

Let's look at a few scriptures:

> *"Be anxious for nothing, but in everything by prayer and supplication, with thanksgiving, let your requests be known to God; and **the peace of God,** which surpasses all understanding, will guard your hearts and minds through Christ Jesus."*
>
> PHILIPPIANS 4:6-7, NKJV (EMPHASIS ADDED)

When your circumstances start to steal your peace, begin thanking God for all He has done and all that He has promised you.

> *"And let **the peace of God** rule in your hearts, to which also you were called in one body; and be thankful."*
>
> COLOSSIANS 3:15, NKJV (EMPHASIS ADDED)

Again, the Holy Spirit ties the peace of God to giving thanks. Thanking God for what He has done requires you to remember all the times God has come through for you. If you are new in faith, read about how God showed up for Daniel in the fiery furnace,[7] for David when facing a giant,[8] for Joshua in front of a high wall.[9]

THE ART OF CONNECTION

Let God's faithfulness encourage you and enable you to be at peace.

GRATITUDE ENTERS YOU INTO GOD'S PRESENCE—

> *"Enter into His gates with **thanksgiving**, and into His courts with praise. Be **thankful** to Him and bless His name!"*
>
> PSALM 100:4, NKJV (EMPHASIS ADDED)

Thankfulness is like a key to the gate of God's presence. Why? Because it takes your focus off you and your problems and puts it where it belongs—on Jesus!

GRATITUDE EVADES ENTITLEMENT—

I'm not sure if all generations that have gone before us feel like the generations coming up have it so much better. Maybe they do. But all generations tend to have a subsection that believes they are entitled to things that are privileges rather than rights. My generation, Gen X, sometimes referred to as "the forgotten generation," has an especially hard time with the entitlement attitude. Gen X'ers patiently waited for the Boomers to pass the baton, only to see that the Boomers wanted to stick around a long time. Long enough for the baton to be passed to the Millennials or Gen Z. And that's why they feel forgotten. Adding insult to injury, some Millennials have an overwhelming sense of entitlement. We (X'ers) think it's because they were raised on too-high doses of positive self-esteem without character or achievement attached.

When we are ungrateful and unloving, we too easily feel like we deserve better than we have and that someone owes it to us.

EXPRESS APPRECIATION DAILY

> *"But know this, that in the last days perilous times will come: For men will be lovers of themselves, lovers of money, boasters, proud, blasphemers, disobedient to parents, **unthankful**, unholy, unloving, unforgiving, slanderers, without self-control, brutal, despisers of good, traitors, headstrong, haughty, lovers of pleasure rather than lovers of God, having a form of godliness but denying its power. And from such people turn away!"*
>
> 2 TIMOTHY 3:1-5, NKJV (EMPHASIS ADDED)

This is one of the Bible's "anti-lists." It's a list that tells you what not to do. What not to be. How not to act. Gratitude helps you avoid this list. You can't overly love yourself if you are thankful for those around you. You can't love money if you recognize who it came from. You won't be disobedient to your parents if you are thankful for them and how much they love you and have done for you.

Expressing gratitude is an antidote to an entitlement attitude. We saw above how a lack of gratitude causes people to have a form of godliness while denying its power. Here, we see that a lack of gratitude causes your thoughts to be futile and your heart to darken:

> *"Because, although they knew God, they did not glorify Him as God, nor were thankful, but became futile in their thoughts, and their foolish hearts were darkened."*
>
> ROMANS 1:21, NKJV

Again, there are two parts to gratitude: recognizing that someone did something for you or gave you something; then expressing and or verbalizing the honor due to that person. These two things together align your thoughts and behavior to avoid entitlement. Gratitude reshapes your paradigm. It causes you to be someone who recognizes God as the giver of all that is good in your life.

> *"Every good and perfect gift is from above, and comes down from the Father of lights, with whom there is no variation or shadow of turning."*
>
> JAMES 1:17, NKJV

GRATITUDE ENGAGES THE POWER OF GOD—

In Luke 17, with the story of the ten lepers—nine Jews and one Samaritan, there are three Greek words used for healing.

- Katharizo—**Cleansed.** *Strong's Concordance* #2511 means to make clean (Luke 17:14).

- Iamai—**Healed.** *Strong's Concordance* #2390 means to heal or cure (Luke 17:15).

- Sozo—**Whole.** *Strong's Concordance* #4982 means to heal, save, deliver, make well, and make whole (Luke 17:19).

Leprosy was a disease that made the Jewish person ceremonially unclean. It deadens the nerve endings in your extremities to where the leper can't feel pain. So, the limbs begin to waste away from fire, rodents, or other untreated injuries. So when Jesus told them to go show themselves to the priests, it was to declare that they

EXPRESS APPRECIATION DAILY

were now ceremonially clean. But they weren't just cleansed; they were healed. Healed and made whole are not the same either. You can be healed of leprosy but still have missing limbs.

When the Samaritan leper saw that he was healed, he ran back to Jesus to show his appreciation. He worshiped Him, glorified God, and thanked Jesus. Then Jesus told him that his faith had made him whole—*Sozo* (v 19). When the Samaritan leper showed his gratitude, he not only received his healing but also was made whole. If he was missing any limbs, the word the author used implied that they grew back. I believe that when this man came back to show his gratitude, his fingers, toes, and limbs were restored. He was cleansed, healed, and whole.

The power of God follows faith. The act of walking to the priest was the leper's faith in action. But then, the Samaritan leper continued to engage that power by giving thanks and worshiping God.

GRATITUDE ENACTS THE WILL OF GOD—

> *"Rejoice always, pray without ceasing, in everything give thanks; **for this is the will of God** in Christ Jesus for you."*
>
> 1 THESSALONIANS 5:16-19, NKJV (EMPHASIS ADDED)

Many people don't understand this verse. It doesn't say that we should give thanks <u>for</u> everything. You don't give thanks for car accidents, failures, loss of jobs, break-ups. No, you give thanks <u>in</u> everything—in the middle of it, during the trial. During whatever circumstance you encounter, thank God for who He is. What He has promised you. What He has already done in your life. That He will work this for your good.

ACCESSING THE BENEFITS IS UP TO US

GRATITUDE IS A LIFESTYLE CHOICE—

You can choose to complain about your circumstances or choose to thank God for who He is—the One who has the power to change your circumstances. When you don't know God's specific will for your life, you can engage in His general will for your life. Engage in gratitude. He is worthy of it all!

Gratitude creates physiological benefits as well as spiritual benefits. It's almost like God gave us a tool to make us happy! Well, not almost. He absolutely gave us this simple tool for a content life. After Paul told the Philippians to be anxious for nothing and with thanksgiving to pray and ask God for their needs,[10] he went on to say, "I have learned to be content whatever the circumstances."[11] The two are connected. Happiness depends on a grateful heart. We just sometimes have to remind ourselves of all the good things God has done for us. When we do, we enjoy all His benefits.

EXPRESS APPRECIATION DAILY

ENDNOTES

1. 1 Thessalonians 5:17-18, NKJV.
2. See James 1:17.
3. See https://www.appreciationatwork.com/5-languages-appreciation-workplace-improve-employee-engagement/.
4. "Gratitude Influences Sleep Through Mechanism of Pre-Sleep Cognitions" by Alex M. Wood, Stephen Joseph, Joanna Lloyd, and Samuel Atkins. Published by the Journal of Psychosomatic Research 66 (2009) 43-48 © 2008. Retrieved from chrome-extension://efaidnbmnnnibpcajpcglclefindmkaj/https://greatergood.berkeley.edu/images/uploads/Wood_et_al._2009_.pdf on April 15, 2025.
5. "Gratitude and Depressive Symptoms: The Role of Positive Reframing and Positive Emotion" by Nathaniel M. Lambert, Frank D. Fincham, and Tyler F. Stillman. Published by Psychology Press © 2011. Retrieved from chrome-extension://efaidnbmnnnibpcajpcglclefindmkaj/https://fincham.info/papers/2011CaE-nate-diss.pdf on April 15, 2025.
6. See Luke 17:11-19.
7. Read Daniel 3 for the account of the fiery furnace.
8. Read 1 Samuel 17 for the account of David and Goliath.
9. Read Joshua 6 for the account of the walls of Jericho falling down.
10. See Philippians 4:6.
11. Philippians 4:11, NIV.

> "Feeling gratitude and not expressing it is like wrapping a present and not giving it."
>
> William Arthur Ward

EXPRESS APPRECIATION DAILY

CHAPTER FIVE
DISCUSSION GUIDE

SUMMARY POINTS

- Gratitude involves both acknowledging what someone has done for you and expressing that appreciation meaningfully.

- People feel appreciated in different ways—through words, time, acts, gifts, or touch—so learn to speak their appreciation language.

- Gratitude provides physical and mental health benefits, such as reducing stress and improving sleep and emotional resilience.

- Spiritually, gratitude draws us closer to God, brings peace, fights entitlement, and engages God's power and presence in our lives.

- Gratitude is a daily decision that aligns us with God's will and opens the door to contentment and joy.

THE ART OF CONNECTION

DISCUSSION QUESTIONS • • • • • • • • • •

1. What's one way someone recently made a difference in your life—and did you express appreciation to them?

2. Which appreciation language(s) do you tend to give in? Which do you best receive?

3. How has gratitude helped you mentally, emotionally, or spiritually in a difficult season?

4. In what areas of life do you struggle with entitlement, and how could gratitude help you reframe those thoughts?

5. How can you make appreciation a more intentional daily habit at home, work, or in your spiritual life?

CHAPTER SIX

FORGIVE QUICKLY

> *"To forgive is the highest, most beautiful form of love. In return, you will receive untold peace and happiness."*
>
> — Robert Muller

Joseph was the eleventh son of Jacob—the first son of Rachel, Jacob's favorite wife, making Joseph his favorite son. Let's save the discussion about the error of having more than one wife for another day. Let's focus on the problems created by Jacob's favoritism of Joseph. The Bible records, "But when (Joseph's) brothers saw that their father loved him more than all his brothers, they hated him and *could not speak peaceably to him.*"[1] You know that someone hates you with a passion when they can't have a conversation with or even speak to you.

Jacob created father wounds in his sons. You are familiar with the story of how the brothers' jealousy of their father's affection made them plot to kill Joseph. Instead, they sold him into slavery. Talk about family wounds. I don't know if I would have waited to see if they had changed if I had the power to put them in prison for

THE ART OF CONNECTION

what they did. Joseph certainly would have been justified. They had basically kidnapped him and sold him to Canaanites. By any court of law, that deserves some jail time.

After selling him, they returned home and lied. They told Jacob that wild animals had killed him, but we know he ended up in Egypt. In an incredible sequence of events that only God could orchestrate, Joseph went from being a slave to second in command next to Pharaoh. During a prolonged famine, Jacob sent the ten older brothers to Egypt to try to buy grain. They did not recognize Joseph, so instead of giving them grain straight away, Joseph toyed with them—I mean, he tested them. (Can you blame him?) He first accused them of being spies, wanting to see if they had changed at all from the conniving, evil men they were who had sold him into slavery. Joseph tested their hearts.

He required that they return home and return with Jacob's youngest son, Benjamin—also a son of Rachel, the favorite wife. Unaware that Joseph knew and understood their language, the brothers talked among themselves about how they had sinned against Joseph, and this was punishment. Moved, Joseph turned away and wept. However much forgiveness and healing had happened in Joseph's heart to that point, there must have been another layer of healing and the gift of closure in hearing those words.

There is much more to the story, and it is worth spending some time reading and reflecting upon it. But for our discussion, we will skip to the part where the brothers were willing to sacrifice their own lives for Benjamin's, both to Joseph (whom they did not yet recognize) and to their father. Once Joseph saw his younger brother, Benjamin, and witnessed the older brothers' changed hearts, he

FORGIVE QUICKLY

revealed himself. In a true display of love, Joseph wept with them and embraced the very people who had cast him away.

Wounds can run deep.

Even wounds that you have forgiven can sometimes leave a scar that can get picked open now and again and cause fresh pain. Require fresh forgiveness. Sometimes, when you are the one receiving the forgiveness, it can be hard to believe you have been forgiven. Something in our nature expects retribution—payback. Guilt and shame have a way of twisting our thoughts into worst-case scenarios and believing anything but the best.

> SOMETIMES, WHEN YOU ARE THE ONE RECEIVING THE FORGIVENESS, IT CAN BE HARD TO BELIEVE YOU HAVE BEEN FORGIVEN.

When Jacob finally lays his head to rest for the last time, we can see one more time the weight of the older brothers' guilt and shame and the depth of Joseph's forgiveness. Fearing that without Jacob present, Joseph would now take his vengeance, the brothers concocted a story. They sent messengers to Joseph, saying their father commanded them to petition Joseph to forgive the brothers and do them no harm. But Joseph answered, "Do not be afraid, for am I in the place of God? But as for you, you meant evil against me; but God meant it for good, in order to bring it about as it is this day, to save many people alive ... and he comforted them and spoke kindly to them."[2]

Joseph understood that only God can take vengeance for the injustice in the world. He alone is just. Before there was a New Testament promise that God works all things together for our good,

THE ART OF CONNECTION

Joseph somehow grasped this reality, too. He was aware there was a bigger picture—a larger story being played out on the canvas of time. He had seen the hand of God at work in every consequence of his brothers' actions against him. Miraculously, Joseph was able to forgive without seeking restitution.

That is a marvelous example, is it not?

WHAT IS FORGIVENESS

So, what is forgiveness? Forgiveness is a banking term that means to release someone from a debt. It's like when a bank releases you from the liability of a mortgage or a car note (which doesn't happen often). They say that the debt is "forgiven."

Most people have trouble forgiving those who hurt them. They demand an apology. They want them to suffer a penalty or provide repayment somehow. Would it surprise you if I told you that forgiveness doesn't require an apology, restitution, or retribution?

Forgiveness is a pardon for the guilty. It is releasing the one who hurt us from their liability to suffer punishment for their crime against us or to have to pay us back.

- Forgiveness is not condoning the behavior of the one who hurt you.
- Forgiveness is not accepting blame for the event.
- Forgiveness does not require that you allow the person back into your life only to be hurt again.
- Forgiveness does not absolve the person of wrongdoing.
- Forgiveness just releases the person from the debt.

FORGIVE QUICKLY

You see, for a bank loan to exist, there must be two parties. The lender and the borrower. As long as the loan exists, both parties are tied to that note. Both are obligated by its terms. However, if the lender forgives the note, they are no longer bound to the terms of the loan. The lender is free.

Forgiveness indeed frees the "borrower" (the offender), but it frees you, too.

Forgiveness means freedom for yourself.

THE COST OF UNFORGIVENESS

When you choose not to forgive someone, anger and resentment build up in your heart. The Bible urges us to pursue peace, or we will end up bitter.

> *"Pursue peace with all people, and holiness, without which no one will see the Lord: looking carefully lest anyone fall short of the grace of God; lest any root of bitterness springing up cause trouble, and by this many become defiled."*
>
> HEBREWS 12:14-15, NKJV

Bitterness defiles. That means bitterness messes things up. It pollutes it, makes it unclean, tarnishes it, and makes it dysfunctional. I heard someone once say that bitterness is like swallowing poison and expecting the other person to die. It is poison.

When we choose not to forgive, we choose not to extend grace. We choose not to bless and not to love as Jesus commands us. You can't move forward if you always rehearse the past hurt and pain. Think of it like this: if someone hit me on the shoulder and caused a bruise, then during my day, someone else inadvertently brushes up against my shoulder. I immediately pull back and wince because it hurts. I might even look at the person who accidentally caused me pain and end up blaming them for the initial wound.

That might sound crazy, but it happens in our lives more often than you might think.

Carrying around bruises and wounds makes it difficult to have close relationships. Think about having a close relationship with someone who just had a car accident. When I was in my early twenties, a guy we knew from street ministry had a car accident. A girl from the church who knew him and I went to visit him in the hospital. You should know that I don't do well with blood. More than once, when put in situations where I see an injury, or like when my wife is giving birth to one of our kids, I tend to black out—faint. This was one of those times.

We walked into the hospital room, and there he was, hooked up to all kinds of machines. His stitches and scars, all over his body, were bloody and scabbing over. The girl with me asked him and his mom, who was sitting beside the bed, if we could pray for him. They agreed, and I began to pray. I finished praying, and then the girl began to pray after me. It wasn't a long prayer from each of us. As soon as she finished, the room started to fade for me. I began to see a black circle around my vision and it was closing. I hurried to walk towards the door, sticking my hand out to feel the frame and guide me into the hall. Once in the hall, my legs gave out. A few minutes later, I could see again, but I was kneeling on the floor several feet away from the hospital room we had just left.

FORGIVE QUICKLY

Most people don't have that kind of reaction to seeing someone bruised, scarred, bloody, and stitched. But most people wouldn't go in for a big hug, either. For one thing, you are afraid you will hurt them—in fact, you expect that you will hurt them unless you keep your distance. There is also a concern that they might get blood on you. Either way, you don't really want to stick around very long.

Bitterness does that. When you have wounds that you carry with you every day, it repels others. Whether you realize it or not, you push people away to keep them at a safe distance. To protect yourself, you think that you are keeping yourself from future hurts. When, in fact, you are robbing yourself of the abundant life that God wants for you.

Go through the process to forgive. It will take some work. Some of it won't be fun, but the resulting freedom is worth it.

HOW TO FORGIVE

It is possible to walk in forgiveness daily. You should walk in forgiveness daily. How do you do this? It is a difficult path, but one that you can travel with God's help. To forgive fully, you must first deal with the spirit of pride. Then, you acknowledge the part you played, release the debtor (offender), and choose to bless them.

1. Confront the spirit of pride.

King Solomon said:

> *"Pride goes before destruction and a haughty spirit before a fall."*
>
> PROVERBS 16:18, NKJV

THE ART OF CONNECTION

When you hold onto the debt, you stand in the place of God and demand justice. When he was the bright and morning star, the archangel Lucifer, he wanted to stand in the place of God. Satan wanted to be exalted, and that pride is what brought him down. Pride will bring you down as well.

The spirit of pride has a twin brother. His name is deception. In order to keep you prideful, this spirit will deceive you into thinking you are right to hold on to the pain. Justified. And you might be, but that doesn't mean it won't hurt you to hang on. But deception will convince you that it is noble to hold on to the debt until it's repaid with a groveling apology. That's what we want, isn't it? We want our abuser or our enemy to grovel with an apology or to at least acknowledge that they have wronged us. Then, we can sit high on a pedestal and release our judgment of, "Guilty!" Wow, that spirit of pride is dangerous. The Prophet Obadiah said, "The pride of your heart has deceived you."[3] Pride keeps you in this place of hurt and pain, so you can't move forward. You rehearse the pain while it festers.

My friend's grandfather one day was hit on the golf course by an errant golf ball from another fairway. It hit him square on the right pectoral muscle. It left a huge black and blue bruise. But the bruise remained for weeks. One day, while telling the story to his grandkids, he made a big motion to show how the ball hit him hard in the chest. When he did so, he used two fingers to pound his chest with a thump. Then he declared, "And I still have the bruise!" My friend shouted, "Papa, you don't have the bruise from the golf ball anymore. That bruise is from you re-telling the story over and over and thumping yourself in the chest!"

FORGIVE QUICKLY

Sometimes, we keep the hurt and pain on life support by rehearsing the event in our minds and telling others how that so-and-so hurt us. With every re-telling, we relive it, making it as fresh in our souls as the day it first happened.

Pride keeps us telling the story to get sympathy and puts us above the offender. We want others to stand as a judge with us. We want them to validate our pain.

Don't let pride keep you from moving forward. Bind it. Bind deception. Keep yourself humble before God, and He will lift you up.[4] God says, "Vengeance is mine; I will repay."[5] You can count on God to keep His promises.

2. **Acknowledge your part.**

After releasing them, or maybe while you are in the process of releasing them, you may have to acknowledge your part in the event that caused your pain. Please do not misunderstand this point. You aren't looking for someone to blame, and you aren't required to take all the blame. You are looking to *learn* from the event. Growth happens through self-awareness. When you can look at the event with objective eyes and see how you could have avoided it or what you might have done differently, if possible, you learn. You grow. Of course, some events can't be mitigated by hindsight. Until others come to your aid or you are old enough to leave, you can't avoid an abusive parent. A sexual assault, a crime, harassment—most of the unavoidable events that cause pain lean towards the extreme. They aren't the everyday offenses that happen. Jesus said, "It is impossible that no offenses should come."[6] These events, the daily ones, usually give us clues that can help us avoid them altogether. What causes offenses, hurts, and wounds between people?

One of the biggest causes of hurt surrounds **unmet expectations.** When I was a kid, my dad would talk about going to Six Flags (an amusement park), or to the lake, or maybe to a baseball game. But then the day would come, and he would change his mind. I'm sure he thought that talking about it wasn't making a promise, but to a ten-year-old, it gave me hope. When he changed his mind, it crushed my hope.

"Don't stop believing!" (to quote Journey). However, we must manage our expectations. Managing your expectations helps you mitigate potential hurts.

Another part of acknowledging your contribution to the offending event involves proximity. Who are you hanging around? Do the people you associate with have high or low integrity? Do you look for signs or clues in people that indicate they keep their word? If you constantly put yourself into a position of relying on unreliable people, that's on you. Proverbs says relying on a fool is like a broken tooth or a bone out of joint.[7] When you do, you are setting yourself up for pain.

3. **Release the debtor.**

When I was about twelve, my dad invited the youth pastor of our church to go water skiing with me and my brother, who was about fourteen. We didn't have a ski boat, but we did have a bass boat that we rigged to pull skiers, and occasionally, we pulled them on this orange sled. The orange sled was a plastic wedge that you could lay on, kneel on, or stand on. It was tied

FORGIVE QUICKLY

to the ski ropes but also had a rope handle on it so you could stand up on the back.

The youth pastor decided he wanted to try the sled while my brother and I acted as spotters. Spotters were the ones looking at the skier who told the driver of the boat when the skier fell or stopped skiing. The youth pastor was older, of course, old to me meant anyone over 20. He looked kind of funny skiing. Remember, this was the 80s, and the swim shorts were short, and the life jackets weren't cool. So there he was on this bright orange sled, standing up on it with the handle.

Somehow, either there was a moment of slack, or there was a turn into a wave, but the front of that sled dipped below the surface. Because it was shaped like a wedge, the water forced it down towards the bottom of the lake. One minute, the youth pastor was there, and the next minute, he was gone! My brother and I didn't make for good spotters because when this happened, we both sat there dumbfounded, in shock. It took a few seconds before we realized we should say something. We both yelled at my dad to stop and waited. A few seconds later, the sled bobbed up to the top like the bobber of a fishing rig. A few seconds after that, the youth pastor emerged in the same manner. We trolled around to pick him up. Once we got him back on the boat, my dad asked him what happened. He said, "I don't know. All of a sudden, I was being dragged underwater. I probably swallowed several gallons of lake water before the thing stopped, and I floated to the surface."

Puzzled, my dad looked at him and asked, "Why didn't you just let go?"

THE ART OF CONNECTION

We often hold on to things too long. We rehearse them in our minds. We wait for the other person to apologize. We live our lives in defeat and hurt. Sometimes, the person who offended us has no idea that they have committed an offense. Like when some wives are upset, and her husband asks her what's wrong and she answers, "If you don't know, then why should I tell you!" It's a losing position to take. Like many husbands, the other person may never know. And it's not because they are cruel or mean or are trying to hurt people. They may just be unaware.

So if someone has offended you, you must tell them. You cannot assume they know. Then, whether or not they are willing to acknowledge the offense, admit wrongdoing, or ask for forgiveness, you must choose to forgive them. For your own spiritual and mental well-being, you must release them from the obligation to make it right with you. Don't stay underwater drowning—just let go.

I know it may sound cruel to tell people who have been abused by parents, sexually assaulted, or worse, to "let it go." I am not trying to oversimplify things—you may need to spend time with a professional therapist or counselor to work through and talk through these issues. Please hear me: I am not condoning the behavior of the other person. And if someone broke the law and committed a crime, they should suffer the consequences to the full extent of the law. What I am saying is that for the benefit of the one who was hurt, letting the pain, anger, and resentment go is the only way to live free.

Choose to forgive, for your sake, for your peace.

FORGIVE QUICKLY

> *"And when you pray, make sure you forgive the faults of others so that your Father in heaven will also forgive you. But if you withhold forgiveness from others, your Father withholds forgiveness from you."*
>
> MATTHEW 6:14-15, TPT

Releasing them—forgiving them isn't for their benefit. It's for you!

4. **Choose to bless them.**

The last part of the forgiveness process tends to be the hardest—choosing to bless them.

> *"But I say to you, love your enemies, bless those who curse you, do good to those who hate you, and pray for those who spitefully use you and persecute you."*
>
> MATTHEW 5:44, NKJV

Choosing to bless the person who offended you may take one statement, and then you move on, or it may take speaking a blessing every time that your anger and resentment come up. Joyce Meyers was sexually abused by her father. She says that you don't know if praying that God would bless them will bless them with truth. Maybe God will show them their sin and bring them to repentance. Again, this part isn't for the offender's benefit. It is for you. For your peace. So you can be made whole.

THE ART OF CONNECTION

Louis Zamperini was an Olympic athlete—a runner. He also enlisted in the military during World War II. During the war in the Pacific, Louis was aboard a plane that was shot down. He and a few others survived the crash but then were adrift in the ocean for forty-seven days. Once they reached the Marshall Islands, they were taken prisoner by the Japanese. As a prisoner, Louis was tortured, beaten, humiliated, starved, and overall terribly mistreated. All of this was over a three-year period until the war ended in 1945.

After the war, Louis had terrible nightmares. He began to drink heavily, becoming an alcoholic. They didn't know much about post-traumatic stress disorder (PTSD) at the time. Most soldiers were expected to tough it out and deal with it. At some point, Louis became engaged, and at her request, Louis attended a Billy Graham crusade. There, he heard the gospel for the first time and gave his life to Jesus. In an interview on the Christian Broadcasting Network in 2003, Louis told the world that the preaching reminded him of his prayers on the life raft, adrift at sea. Following his born-again experience, he forgave his captors.

His nightmares finally stopped.

He didn't stop there. Graham helped him begin a new career as a Christian evangelist. His life message was forgiveness. He visited some of the guards of his prison camp. Many had been arrested as war criminals. Some of them became Christians because Louis didn't just forgive them. Sharing Jesus with his former captors blessed them with eternal life.

FORGIVE QUICKLY

Many counselors will tell you that you should forgive. But Jesus asks us to go just a bit further and bless. You can't have anger and resentment in your heart when you purpose to bless.

FORGIVING GOD

There is one last thing to discuss before we close this chapter—who do you need to forgive? Painful events surrounding people make it a bit easier to discern who to forgive. But sometimes, there isn't a person involved. Disappointments and offenses can occur when a loved one dies, when we lose a job, when a leader falls, or just when we don't get what we expected (or prayed for). Sometimes, the blame for those events falls squarely on God's shoulders. It's not that God deserves the blame. No, that usually falls somewhere else. Unfortunately, it is human nature to get angry and bitter towards the One who loves you the most. We do not have the benefit of standing outside of time. We cannot see the end from the beginning. We cannot comprehend how God can possibly work some of the hard things we endure for our good.

But He can.

He will.

I once shared my faith with someone I knew in high school. She was a wife and mother of a few kids. During the conversation, she shared why she didn't believe in God. She had worked as a child advocate and read a police report about what some idiot had done to some children. Her question was not unlike one that many people ask: "How could a loving God allow such atrocities to happen? If

THE **ART** OF **CONNECTION**

God is all-powerful, why doesn't He stop this tragedy from ever occurring?"

It's a fair question and one that deserves an honest answer.

The better question would be, "How do we see any good in the world?" When sin entered the world, it corrupted every part. God set man on the earth and gave him dominion over it. We had legal title and authority on the earth to make it a paradise as God had intended. But when Adam gave his authority over to Satan, that's when sin and evil entered the world like a virus, corrupting everything.

Bad things happen because the thoughts of man's heart have become evil. The fact that there is any good in the world is because God sent His Word, Jesus, to save the world. That through Him, we might be a light to the world.

If you have blamed God for some evil that a human being did to you or because of negative circumstances, please forgive Him. Remember, forgiving brings **you** freedom. It releases the other person from the obligation to "make it right." God has already done everything necessary to bring you abundant life. He sent Jesus to die for our sin and to rise from the dead so that anyone who believes that He is alive and makes Him Lord over their life will be saved. God sent the Holy Spirit so that we can commune with Him and live a righteous and good life.

His plans for you are good. His promises are true. He is working on your behalf even when you cannot see it or feel it—even when circumstances look impossible or cruel. God loves you with an everlasting love, and He will be faithful to complete the work He began in you. I cannot begin to explain, much less comprehend,

FORGIVE QUICKLY

the mysteries of His way or how He will ensure that in the span of eternity, He will work all things for my good.

But I know it to be true. I trust the finished work of Christ. I trust that His forgiveness of me is so great that I have no real right not to extend my forgiveness to others—and to Him.

Forgiving God will free you from resentment and bitterness that stop the flow of God's grace into your life.

> *"When you forgive, you in no way change the past—but you sure do change the future."*
>
> BERNARD MELTZER

ENDNOTES

1. Genesis 37:4, NKJV.
2. Genesis 50:19-21, NKJV.
3. Obadiah 3a, NKJV.
4. See James 4:10.
5. See Romans 12:19.
6. Luke 17:1a, NKJV.
7. See Proverbs 25:19.

THE ART OF CONNECTION

Forgiveness means
freedom for yourself.

FORGIVE QUICKLY

CHAPTER SIX
DISCUSSION GUIDE

SUMMARY POINTS

- Forgiveness is releasing someone from the debt of offense, not because they deserve it, but to free yourself from bitterness and pain.

- Unforgiveness leads to emotional, relational, and spiritual toxicity, often harming the offended more than the offender.

- Forgiveness is a process that includes confronting pride, acknowledging your part, releasing the offender, and blessing them.

- Forgiving does not excuse harmful behavior or require restored relationship—it simply removes your obligation to seek retribution.

- Resentment toward God due to pain or disappointment must also be addressed through forgiveness, which restores peace and trust.

THE ART OF CONNECTION

DISCUSSION QUESTIONS • • • • • • • • • •

1. Is there someone you've forgiven in your head but not yet in your heart? What's still holding you back?

2. How has unforgiveness affected your physical, emotional, or spiritual well-being?

3. Which step in the forgiveness process (confront pride, acknowledge your part, release, bless) do you find most challenging, and why?

4. Have you ever felt the need to forgive God? What helped you move through that process?

5. What can you do today to begin living in daily forgiveness and walk in greater peace?

CHAPTER SEVEN

LEARN TO LISTEN

VALUE WHAT OTHERS HAVE TO SAY

To get along with people, you must value them. That means valuing what they have to say. Active listening goes beyond just sitting in front of someone while they talk. Active listening involves paying attention to the whole person—what they say (cognitive), what they feel (emotional), and what they do (behavioral). If you misinterpret any one of those areas, you run the risk of misunderstanding the speaker. Misunderstandings lead to conflict. Almost every sitcom focuses on some form of misunderstanding.

I remember watching some as a kid and thinking, *these people do the same thing every week.* One character takes what someone said or did the wrong way, and they spend the next thirty minutes hilariously trying to solve a problem that doesn't exist. Many authors have made a good living on this common human flaw. It's funny when it's someone else's problem. But when it's you and your co-workers or you and your friends, the humor sometimes disappears.

THE ART OF CONNECTION

To avoid living in your own terrible 80's sitcom, let's dive deeper into how we can actively listen to truthfully understand the people around us.

What do we normally do when someone talks? Most of us think about our response or think about a situation that we encountered that sounds similar to what they are describing. It takes time to train yourself not to do those things. To listen closely to what the other person says solely for the point of understanding them requires patience and empathy.

A few weeks ago, I told my wife that I wasn't feeling well. She immediately talked about how she hadn't felt well and all the things that felt off to her that day. To her, that is making a connection with me through our shared experiences. To me, she was trying to one-up me and steal the attention that I was clearly trying to get from her. We have laughed about this before. I reminded her of this, and then she asked me more about how I was feeling. We've been married for 29 years, so I know she loves me and cares about how I feel. But others you encounter may not.

Do your best not to one-up the speaker. That takes away the attention from them. Not everyone attempts to gain attention like I do from my wife. Others are genuinely expressing themselves to you by sharing their experience. A better response than giving them one of your stories would be to ask a question showing that you heard them and want more information.

For most of my life, I thought when people brought their problems to me, they wanted a solution. This couldn't be further from the truth. I am a problem solver by nature. I enjoy problems just for the opportunity to solve them—except when it's in a math class for

LEARN TO LISTEN

some kind of grade. Then it's not as fun. I have learned that the proper response to someone's mind dump of their problem or experience would be, "Wow, what do you think about that?" or "Huh, that sucks." Without passing judgment or criticizing their behavior or response, just nod your head. Offering unsolicited advice sometimes comes off as critical or judgmental. We have discussed being critical already, so I won't expand on it here.

> OFFERING UNSOLICITED ADVICE SOMETIMES COMES OFF AS CRITICAL OR JUDGMENTAL.

CURIOSITY IS A SUPERPOWER

Still, active listening in the cognitive area requires curiosity. My mom used to say, "Curiosity killed the cat!" I had no idea what she meant. Maybe that's where my disdain for cats comes from, or maybe it's because I'm allergic. I don't know. Anyway, **curiosity is a good thing.** In a mystery, or on *Scooby Doo,* it will either get you into trouble or solve the mystery. It could go either way. But in conversations with real people, curiosity shows genuine concern. It asks more questions to gain understanding. Those questions also make the speaker feel valued.

Several months ago, I went to an estate sale. I love garage sales and estate sales. The hunt to find value where others see junk makes me happy. At this estate sale, I looked for books, guns, and other collectibles. I found a box of comic books. About 60 to 70 of them. They were asking for two dollars per book. I asked them if they would take $60 for the whole lot. They agreed, and I walked away with the beginning of a collection. When I got back to my house I looked up each one on eBay. Most were selling for a few dollars, some even up

THE **ART** OF **CONNECTION**

to $20, a few up to $100. But if that wasn't good enough, there was a half-sized comic book that sold on eBay for $495! I could hardly believe my good fortune! But then I saw that my box of comics had three of those half-sized books that were identical! My $60 investment had turned into close to $2,000 in value.

I found value in that estate sale *because I looked for it.*

When you talk to someone, be a person who looks for value. When you value people, you want to know more about them and their experiences. A curious person sees people as potential value to discover. Not to be used, but to be cherished. Does that sound too Hallmark Christmas Movie to you? It might, but it's true nonetheless. Jesus valued people. When He looked on them, He had compassion for them.[1]

A wise leader, a good friend, someone who wants to get along with others discovers the value in others. They draw it out like throwing a pail into a deep well and pulling the pail up so everyone can take a drink.

> *"Counsel in the heart of man is like deep water,
> but a man of understanding will draw it out."*
>
> PROVERBS 20:5

Another part of active listening requires you to interpret the tone or emotions of the speaker. This is part of the message coding. Someone can say that they are fine, your wife perhaps, yet they are NOT fine! Emotional cues take some skill to detect. I highly recommend that you rely on the Holy Spirit to guide you in understanding. You have to listen between the lines sometimes.

LEARN TO LISTEN

I had the privilege of going to India a few months ago. I still wonder how I ended up going on this trip. It was supposed to be a discovery trip to see what kind of business ventures I might create. While I was there, I was able to speak to some students at a leadership college. The week I went, the country prepared for elections coming in the fall. For me, that didn't mean much since the work I did had favor with the government. However, the man in charge of the leadership college had concerns about me traveling from the hotel to the school. The police were doing random stops. Well, I got stopped on one of the last days of my trip. My driver that day hadn't driven me before and didn't speak much English. The police tapped on my window and asked me to step out of the car. Or, that's what the driver said he wanted. They brought me back to the back of the car where my luggage was, fully packed for my return trip to the U.S. One officer had a video camera (Like the one my father-in-law had in the late 90s—a VHS. It looked like a small suitcase on his shoulder).

The officer in charge motioned toward my suitcase. The driver said he wanted me to open it. I pulled the zippers back and one half was exposed where you could see my shirts and pants folded tightly and held by straps. The other side was zipped closed. The officer looked at it and motioned toward it. I got the gist of what he wanted. I began to unzip that side while that half of the suitcase was still propped up vertically. As the corner flap of the cover came open, my underwear started falling out into the other part of the suitcase. Immediately, the officer told me to stop and zip it back up. I didn't understand his language, but he clearly didn't want to see any more of my dirty clothes, especially my undergarments.

Learning emotional cues can seem like learning a foreign language. Even in India, I could get an idea from the context of what

THE ART OF CONNECTION

the officer wanted from me. But interacting with people everyday, we sometimes overlook the emotional cues. I used to tell my staff to listen to how people feel as much or more than what they say. Emotional states make us say things we don't mean and sometimes say things that contradict our feelings.

> EMOTIONAL STATES MAKE US SAY THINGS WE DON'T MEAN AND SOMETIMES SAY THINGS THAT CONTRADICT OUR FEELINGS.

Emotional cues come from body language, tone, volume, and our pace. I'm not an expert in these cues. More of an amateur sleuth. A hobbyist detective who, for the sake of survival in this complex world, learned a few things by trial and error. There are some great articles on emotional cues in communication all over the internet. I haven't read any of them. *Just kidding.* I've read a few, and for the most part, it is a guessing game. One of the best books I've read about emotional cues was written for authors who wanted to improve how they depicted their character's emotions. It's called *The Emotion Thesaurus: A Writer's Guide to Character Expression* by Angela Ackerman and Becca Puglisi.

While this book teaches writers how to convey their character's unique emotions, it describes what the face, the heart, and the hands do when people are mad, sad, happy, etc. It's a good resource for the socially awkward person who doesn't instinctively read people's emotional signs. Also, if you want to write a novel, it can be a handy tool.

LEARN TO LISTEN

COMMUNICATION DIAGRAM

The Communication Diagram allows us to see the process of communication. Here is a simple rendering.

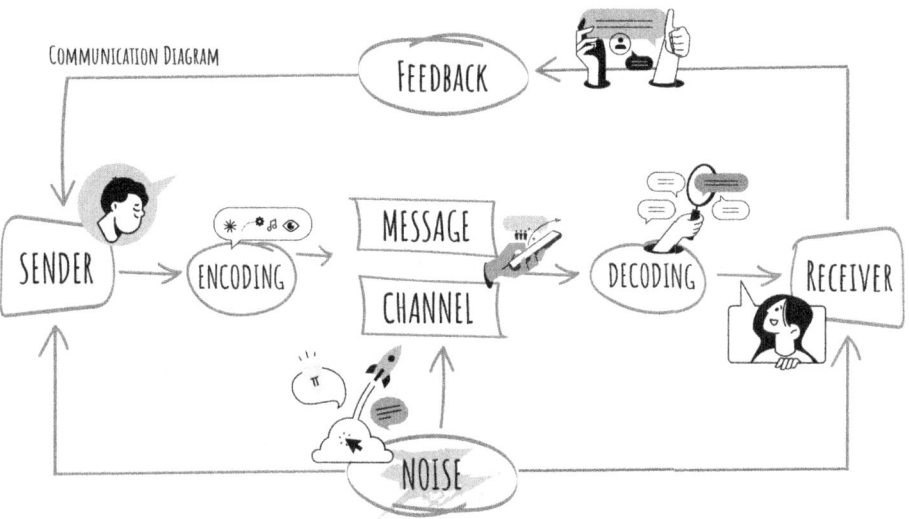

In this diagram, you see that, for communication to take place, there must be a sender and a receiver. The sender sends a message. How that message is sent is its channel. Before the message is sent, the sender chooses the encoding—or the language of the message. The receiver must accept the channel that the message rides along. That means he must pay attention, accept the phone call, go to where the message will be delivered, or read the text. The action of reading the text or listening to the message in a language the receiver understands is decoding.

But wait, there's more. All of that message must pass through noise—the potential distractions the receiver may encounter. Once the message has been received and decoded, the final part of

THE ART OF CONNECTION

communication is feedback. Feedback is the receiver acknowledging that they have received and understood the message.

You may not have known all that was happening when you sent your mom a text or talked to your friend at work. But indeed, communication is a complex process.

If you have ever played the game "Telephone," you know that sometimes the message can get distorted the more it's filtered from person to person. In Telephone, you whisper a message to the first person in line. Usually, you have at least ten people. That person who received the secret message, maybe "The Cowboys are going to dominate the Giants this season," turns to the next person in line and repeats what they heard. This process is repeated until you get to the tenth person. The last person then announces the message to compare it to what the first person said. Each participant cannot ask questions to the person who told them the message. They must immediately turn and whisper the message they heard to the next person. Usually, by the end of the line, the message comes out distorted. Maybe something like, "All boys demonstrate giant reasons?"

So what happened? You had a sender and receiver, both presumably spoke English and delivered the message along a channel that is common to each participant? We don't always hear exactly what the sender sends. And without feedback or asking questions, our brain fills in the missing parts of the message before we share that message with the next person. Also, the channel chosen, word of mouth, lends itself to misinterpretation. But the best players of the game know that they aren't required to tell the exact message. If they want, they can replace the names of the teams or say something completely different. In your relationships, if that's happening, you have bigger

LEARN TO LISTEN

problems that have bigger names, like triangulation, manipulation, and gaslighting—but this book isn't about that!

Each part of communication has its challenges. So, let's go through each part and describe ways to bring clarity to our messaging and interactions with people.

THE SENDER—

When you look at communication, you should begin with the motives and integrity of the sender. Like in the game Telephone, the sender can choose to honor the rules of the game or attempt to deliberately deceive the receiver in the wrong direction. In our world of the twenty-four-hour news cycle, we must be aware of the motives behind the message. It used to be the motto of journalists to report the news. Now, when you ask a journalist why they got into that line of work, they say, "To change the world!" Unfortunately, this internal bias will pervade every message of that "journalist." So when you receive news from Facebook, TikTok, Instagram, or actual news sources, ask yourself, "What is the sender's motivation?" It matters. Most want to persuade you to their point of view. Some don't exude much integrity in the process. Certainly, many believe the ends justify the means. So consider the sender when you interpret the message.

THE MESSAGE—

The message sent by the sender may be in many forms. The sender must choose the language and vehicle in which to deliver it. Since the encoding by the sender and the decoding by the receiver may be different, the sender should take measures to make the message as clear and unambiguous as possible. Easier said than done.

THE **ART** OF **CONNECTION**

Clarity is the single most important part of the message. What can dilute clarity? We discussed earlier the emotional cues that people give during conversations. An angry face saying pleasant words easily taints the message the receiver decodes. Sarcasm is another example.

> CLARITY IS THE SINGLE MOST IMPORTANT PART OF ANY MESSAGE.

A written message versus a spoken message can help to bring clarity, but it can still miss the mark by not considering your tone. When my kids were younger, they would receive texts from me and think I was mad at them. Why? Because I used punctuation in my texts. For them, you only used punctuation when you were upset or making a point. For me, using punctuation implied professionalism. When texting clients, if I used slang or abbreviations, my clients would wonder if they had the right person for their tax or financial services work. Once I explained my habit, they didn't feel like my texts were getting on to them. And, I started to leave off the punctuation at the end of a text just to put them at ease.

A text or an email won't convey your tone—unless you use emojis. However, using emojis with professional emails and texts is sometimes frowned upon depending on the business relationship and how close the users might be. With my firm, the staff never used email to resolve a conflict. We set up a meeting or had a phone call. Conflict resolution requires you to empathize with the participants. Email does not exude much empathy. Someone may be sincere, but their ability to compose a written message may not allow that sincerity to come through.

LEARN TO LISTEN

THE RECEIVER—

Knowing your receiver—your audience—makes all the difference when forming your message. Before writing a book, a speech, or an email, always think about the audience. The more specific your audience, the more tailored your message should be.

For example, I write my books for young adults. If you read this book as an old adult, please don't feel like it isn't for you. However, I write books that are designed to help guide young people in life through the challenges I have faced. I hope they don't make the same mistakes I did in money, business, and relationships. That's my general audience. But I recommend going further and forming your message to one person. Create an avatar of the audience you want to connect with. How old are they? Do they go to church? Are they married? Do they have children? Where do they live? What kind of car do they drive? Do they drive? These are a few of the questions you might ask. Then, think of a person you might know who fits all those criteria, or at least most of them. If you don't know someone, then give that person a name.

When you know your audience, you know how they will respond to your message. It'll also dictate what language you use to convey that message. Will they allow contractions, like I just used? Will they require technical language to take you seriously, like at a tax accountant conference?

> **WHEN YOU KNOW YOUR AUDIENCE, YOU KNOW HOW THEY WILL RESPOND TO YOUR MESSAGE.**

THE ART OF CONNECTION

FEEDBACK—

The receiver (listener), while the message is being conveyed, should give cues to the sender that they understand. This part of the communication diagram is feedback. Feedback comes in lots of forms. Sometimes verbal, like saying yes or uh-huh and nodding your head. Feedback cues the sender that what they say makes sense or does not make sense. For the comedian, laughter means things are going well. Silence means things are definitely not going well.

Feedback becomes the listener's message to the sender. It has its own encoding, channel, and decoding. At our church, the congregation generally gives feedback pretty well. A few "Amens!" here and there, laughter at the right time, smiling and bobbing of heads. Well, our pastor went to preach at another congregation recently. It was full of young people who were from many different countries. A very international group. They were basically silent for most of the message. He didn't know if they were getting much out of it. Afterward, he spoke to a few and found out that most of them had been taking furious notes. Almost transcribing the message. Their method of feedback wasn't verbal cues but note-taking. If the pastor had looked closely while speaking he would have noticed the scribbling in notebooks the entire message!

Some ways to give feedback are asking curious probing questions, mirroring body language, summarizing the conversation, repeating the questions or statements, making eye contact, taking notes, and verbal affirmations.

We will talk about asking curious, probing questions later as a means to deepen relationships. Here, we will mention how a curious question can make the speaker feel appreciated and communicate interest. Asking questions shows that you are engaged in the conversation and are trying to understand the speaker.

It can also show that you don't understand the speaker. Asking questions helps to bring clarity and assures that the speaker and the listener understand each other.

EMPATHY IN COMMUNICATION

Years ago, someone wise once said that we judge others on their actions, but we judge ourselves on our intentions. Why do we do this? Well, because we walk around in our own shoes. We have easy access to our thoughts and know that actions come from the seed of our thoughts and emotions. So, how do we begin to live out a life of empathy? We have to learn, as the cliché goes, to put ourselves in someone else's shoes. Let's first define empathy.

Webster's Online Dictionary defines empathy as the action of understanding, being aware of, being sensitive to, and vicariously experiencing the feelings, thoughts, and experiences of another. That's a big job for people. Many do this instinctively. There was even a character on *Star Trek: Next Generation* who claimed to be an empath. Someone who supernaturally was able to sense the feelings and intentions of others. Well, you don't have to be part alien or have supernatural gifting to improve your empathy game. From practice, you can become more aware, gain understanding, and learn to be more sensitive to the thoughts, feelings, and experiences of others.

To grow in empathy requires that you first practice awareness. There's a spiritual movement going on that focuses on being mindful. Mindfulness practitioners seek to be at peace with the world by being in the moment and sensing things around them. That is not what I'm talking about. What I'm talking about relates more to situational awareness—reading the room. Becoming aware of how people feel. Looking for their emotional cues. I can get pretty focused on my tasks and the vision of the organization rather than paying attention to people. Early in my career as a tax accountant, I would ignore emotional cues and do my best to avoid them. My mantra at the time was, "Leave your problems at the door; we are here to do a job!" And it wasn't just my mantra. Many businesses treat their employees like this. Unfortunately, as a leader, you can't ignore what people are feeling and experiencing. It will impact every message they send and receive.

To this day, I don't really know how to respond when someone cries in my office. Even as a pastor now, I get uncomfortable. But that's a self-centered response. I've learned to bring the tissue box over and sit with the person. You don't really have to say anything.

> THE PRACTICE OF EMPATHY SEES THE EMOTIONS AND THEN TRIES TO PUT YOURSELF IN THEIR SHOES TO UNDERSTAND WHAT THEY FEEL.

Emotions happen to us. They are valid, and they shouldn't be ignored. Ignoring those emotions ignores the identity of the person sitting in front of you. The practice of empathy sees the emotions and then tries to put yourself in their shoes to understand what they feel.

We will never completely understand how others feel until we experience what they experience. Yet, we can imagine being in their place and allowing ourselves to feel what they feel. It's not just sympathy. **Sympathy is feeling for someone,** feeling bad for another's misfortune. While sympathy acknowledges someone's situation,

LEARN TO LISTEN

it makes no effort to understand. Sympathy is the surface, polite response to the emotions felt by others. It doesn't require awareness or understanding. Sympathy doesn't build connection with people. **Empathy is feeling with someone.** Empathy builds those connections. When you become aware of the emotions and feelings and understand the other person's experience, you attempt to view it from their perspective, and you connect on a deeper level.

Think of sympathy as observing and acknowledging and empathy as connecting and understanding.

REMOVING DISTRACTIONS

Often people will come into my office and want to visit about an issue that is important to them. They might sit in the chairs in front of my desk or, now, on the couch across the room. It has been my habit now for some time to get up out of my desk chair, walk around the desk, and sit near them to listen. I used to try to have meetings at my desk. Unfortunately, my desk contains many distractions. My laptop, if open, may announce a new email has arrived. Or my notes from my previous meeting may stare at me and want me to think about how to solve that issue instead of the one my teammate just brought to my attention. My phone on my desk may display a new text or chat message. So. Many. Distractions!

Just now, I had to stop and send a few texts just to get some peace. In conversations with friends and family, distractions may be allowed occasionally. People tend to have a lot of grace about the interruption from our cell phones a lot more than they used to. I think that's a bit sad. I have a friend who, every time we go to lunch or have a meeting, gets a few texts that always seem to be more important. He doesn't know that he is conveying that message. But when everyone

THE ART OF CONNECTION

in the room has to wait for you to reply, the message is loud and clear: YOU AREN'T THAT IMPORTANT!

That may seem harsh, but respect for people includes respecting their time. When you take someone to lunch, you say to them that you want that time to be separated for just them. Allowing your phone to interrupt that time erodes that connection.

Just after I got my smartwatch, I had a meeting with one of my favorite clients. We talked about their portfolio and how it responded to the current market. I kept getting texts from people during that meeting. Even though I had left my phone on my desk and was visiting with them around a table set up for these meetings, I still got distracted. My client asked if I had somewhere to go. Confused, I looked at her and said, "No, why?" She said, "You keep looking at your watch." Embarrassed, I apologized. I told her and her husband I just bought the smart watch, and I hadn't learned how to turn the notifications off.

I still get the notifications on my watch. I have just learned how to ignore them. That's what we have to do when we listen to others. We have to learn to ignore the notifications. Dial in, stay engaged, be focused ... whatever term you want to use. But the thing we must remember to do is pay attention.

In the communication diagram we looked at before, Noise represents the distractions around the conversation. Noise might be internal or external. Internally, you may get distracted by your weekly to-do list, a conversation with your spouse, or your boss' facial expression you didn't understand from yesterday's staff meeting.

External distractions range from other people, the slides behind the speaker, a fly buzzing around your head. The list is

LEARN TO LISTEN

immeasurable as to the external distractions. So, what can you do to stay focused?

- **Take notes.** What tells a speaker or your co-worker that what they say has meaning and value to you? When you write it down. You can use an iPad or a pen and paper. I went to a client meeting without my notebook, thinking it would be just a meet and greet. Then, the client started telling me all the things they needed help with. I took out my phone to take notes. But before I did, I told him, "I'm taking notes on my phone, not texting while you speak." Even though I told him that, I could tell it made him a bit uncomfortable. It would have been better to get out my laptop or ask for a pen and paper.

- **Give verbal affirmations.** In church, when I preach, I love to hear people comment back, "Yes!" or "Amen!" It makes a preacher feel like they hit a home run. In your conversations at work or in meetings, it is perfectly okay to give a subtle "Uh-huh" to affirm the speaker. Though, in a business meeting, I'm pretty sure a hearty "Amen!" might get you some funny looks.

- **Make eye contact.** My pastoral team at church engaged in some training for pastoral care at our offices. The trainer asked us to get into pairs and face each other. We were asked to stare at each other for two minutes. That felt unbelievably awkward. I didn't know where to look. Deep into his eyes or at his ears, or the space between his eyebrows? That's not what we want here. Eye contact affirms to the speaker that they have your full attention. You can break away occasionally and maybe blink some to keep the speaker from feeling stared down. Make a mental note of their eye color. That's a good trick to make sure you are actually engaged in eye contact.

- **Mirror.** Mirroring the speaker's body language puts the speaker at ease. It helps with keeping your attention as well. I don't recommend the mirroring that a mime might do in the park. If the speaker leans forward in their chair, they may be excited about the topic. To show that you are also excited about the topic, you should lean forward as well. If the speaker is relaxed and crosses their legs while leaning back. You can also relax some.

- **Repeat back and summarize.** These two actions relay to the speaker that you understand what they are saying. Repeating back says the same thing as the speaker, nearly word for word, while summarizing puts in your words what you heard. Both help the speaker feel like you hear them and understand them. If you summarize and it doesn't represent what the speaker intended, then the speaker has the opportunity to clarify what they said.

- **Ask clarifying questions.** We will talk about all kinds of questions later that help you get along with anyone, anywhere. Here, we ask questions to bring clarity. In his book, *The Four Obsessions of an Extraordinary Executive*, Patrick Lencioni emphasizes the importance of clarity in an organization. Two of the four obsessions revolve around clarity. If you don't have a clear target, you won't hit the mark. In a conversation, or meeting, or public speaking event, you need to have a clear objective. Clarifying questions by the listener helps the speaker to focus their message. Clarifying questions may ask for details, or they may ask for what to

LEARN TO LISTEN

do next. Asking clarifying questions helps you to stay in the conversation as well as give you more information.

These conversation tools will help you stay focused and overcome the distractions that occur whenever a message needs to be heard.

THE FIFTH HABIT

In Steven Covey's book, *The Seven Habits of Highly Effective People,* the fifth habit states that we should seek to understand rather than to be understood. I highly recommend you read that book, paying special attention to that chapter.

Learning to listen depends on this habit. The mindset of every active listener should be to understand. To understand someone, you must avoid a few things. You should avoid framing your response while they speak—trust me, this is a hard habit to break! You should also avoid forming judgments about what they say and avoid interjecting your opinions before they finish speaking. All of those things are easier said than done, but all will make an incredible leap forward in your efforts to get along with anyone.

With practice and patience, you can learn to listen well. As we stated at the beginning of this chapter, when we value people, we listen to them. If you wait to speak rather than try to understand, you take away their identity. They no longer exist as a person. They instead become an obstacle to be overcome.

Use the techniques in this chapter to actively listen to others and become someone others will want to be around. Before I grew up and started having a bunch of opinions and pride in myself, I had some people tell me they liked being around me. They said that I made them feel important. I'm not sure when I lost that quality. But

THE **ART** OF **CONNECTION**

I know I did. Unfortunately, it took me years to figure out it was lost and worth finding again.

What do you want others to say about you? I know we aren't supposed to care about what others say about us, but the Bible says, "The fear of man brings a snare, but trust in the Lord and you will be safe."[2] Yes, we shouldn't let what others say about us dictate our lives and keep us in fear about what we do or how we act. Yet, what others say about our character has value.

The Bible instructs that we shouldn't judge lest we be judged.[3] True. But it also says you will know a tree by its fruit.[4] As a pastor once said, "We may not be people judges, but we are fruit inspectors." Only God knows the thoughts and intents of the heart. But your friends and family can see the results of your behavior. You can see the results of your behavior. The fruit.

> *"But the fruit of the Spirit is love, joy, peace, patience, kindness, goodness, faithfulness, gentleness, and self-control."*
>
> GALATIANS 5:22-23A, NASB

When we allow the Holy Spirit to lead us and allow his character to come through, people will notice. By combining the insights of this chapter plus relying on the Holy Spirit's guidance, you can become someone others want to be around.

ENDNOTES

1. See Matthew 9:36, 14:14, and 15:32.
2. Proverbs 2:25, NKJV.
3. See Matthew 7:1.
4. See Matthew 7:15-20.

LEARN TO LISTEN

CHAPTER SEVEN DISCUSSION GUIDE

SUMMARY POINTS

- Active listening involves paying attention to what someone says, feels, and does—and communicates that you value them.

- Genuine curiosity helps you draw out the best in others and fosters deeper, more meaningful conversations.

- Empathy, not just sympathy, allows you to feel with others, read emotional cues, and build authentic connections.

- Clear communication requires feedback, elimination of distractions, and intentional focus on both message and tone.

- Listening to understand rather than respond reflects spiritual maturity and allows the fruit of the Spirit to be seen in your life.

THE ART OF CONNECTION

DISCUSSION QUESTIONS

1. In your daily conversations, do you tend to listen to understand or to respond? Why?

2. How can you better recognize and respond to emotional cues in others?

3. What distractions do you need to eliminate to become a better listener at work or home?

4. How might curiosity improve your relationships?

5. Which listening skill or habit do you most want to grow in—and what's one way to start practicing it this week?

CHAPTER EIGHT

ASK CURIOUS QUESTIONS

SO MANY QUESTIONS!

> "Now so it was that after three days they found Him in the temple, sitting in the midst of the teachers, both listening to them and asking them questions."
>
> LUKE 2:46, NKJV

As we discussed in "Learn to Listen," active listening includes asking clarifying questions. But questions do much more than clarify or help the listener understand. Many times questions help lead people to awareness.

To get along with others we need a lot of self-awareness. Self-awareness leads us to others-awareness, which helps us understand the people around us. Using questions instead of statements helps us to gain that awareness and understanding.

In one of my favorite sitcoms, one of the characters tells us going into an interview that he will answer every question with a question.

THE **ART** OF **CONNECTION**

The interviewer asks, "Were you aware that the teachers were invited to the dinner?"

The interviewee answers, "Would I have gone if I did?"

"I don't know, would you?"

"Would you have gone?

Those are not the kind of questions I'm advocating for here, although it sounds like a fun experiment. What I hope you do is cultivate curiosity. When you meet people, ask questions!

A few years ago, I noticed that when someone asked me how I was doing, I always answered, "Great, thank you." But somehow, I didn't think to ask them how they were doing. This seems small, but I realized how self-centered that was. Those asking may have thought I didn't ask because I didn't care. But that wasn't the case. I did care, but I had such tunnel vision that my mind was always focused on my next task.

Take time to ask. But don't stop at asking, "How are you doing?" People love talking about themselves. It's true. It's everyone's favorite topic. (I know my extroverts are wondering why bother with this list, but the introverts are taking notes.) Here's a list of questions that you can cycle through in a few minutes that help others feel like you care:

1. **How is your family?** If you know someone specifically, put their name in there. People love to talk about their family. If they don't have family, ask about their pets.

2. **What are you working on?** For someone like me who has several projects going at the same time, you may have opened the door to a thirty-minute conversation, but it's worth the

ASK CURIOUS QUESTIONS

risk. Lots of people have hobbies that they are itching to talk about. Sometimes, this question will bring that out.

3. **What are you doing after this?** This is a great all-purpose question. This question could pertain to college, or a class, or just lunch.

4. **What do you think about _____?** Insert the topic of your choice. The key here is to be relevant to the person you are talking to. It would help to know a little about them before using this question, but if you have asked about their family and their work, that might provide you with clues about what to ask here.

5. **What books are you reading right now?** This one only works for bookworms like me. I love to talk about books. Fiction or non-fiction. It doesn't matter. I'm always looking for my next read, and other readers like to talk about their books as well.

6. **What podcasts are you listening to, or what are you watching that has your interest?** So, if they turn out not to be avid readers, this is a question you can pivot to. It will help you gain insight into who they are, what they like, and help you connect more meaningfully.

These questions may seem a bit cheesy to you, but they work to start conversations. Having follow-up questions ready will help the introvert keep the conversation going. But usually, once one of these starters comes up, the conversation will keep rolling. Be sure to listen for understanding, not just to cue up your next question, or it will feel more like an interrogation than a conversation!

THE ART OF CONNECTION

CULTIVATING CURIOSITY

Staying curious means you *really* want to know more than you do. It comes from a place of humility. Know-it-alls don't ask curious questions. If they ask a question, it's because they think they know the answer. Being curious begins with a humble spirit.

A few years ago, I took piano lessons. I remember walking into the music school for the first time. I was surrounded by kids waiting, some with their parents, others alone, for their lessons to begin. I sat down, wondering what I was doing there. It felt a bit ridiculous being in my late forties waiting for my lesson. I had been forced to take lessons as a kid. From third grade to fifth grade, I walked from our house down the street to our piano teacher's house once a week. She played the piano and organ for our small Southern Baptist church in Irving, Texas. It was incredibly boring to me then. I had no desire to play the piano at that time. My parents had to threaten me with beatings just to get 30 minutes of practice from me each day. After those three years, I had a small grasp of music theory but could not play anything recognizable. The next year, I played trombone in junior high. Then, I quit music altogether for a few years.

As kids, we don't always understand the value of what we learn. At nineteen, I picked up the guitar and began to play songs using lead sheets that had the chords above the lyrics. It was a lot more fun to learn that way. I played every day, practicing and learning new chords. My desire and passion for music made the difference.

Twenty years later, I wanted to learn the piano. But this time, I wanted to learn the way I learned to play the guitar. By learning chords so that I could play songs immediately. But before I could.

ASK CURIOUS QUESTIONS

I had to walk into a music school filled with kids. I had to humble myself so that I could learn.

That's what curiosity does. It opens your mind and heart to the possibility of learning something new. People are enigmas waiting to be figured out. Every person you come in contact with has a story. Their story is unique. It may have some similarities to your story or someone you know, but it is their personal story. My brother and I are only twenty-two months apart in age. We grew up in the same town in the same house for most of our childhood. Yet, with all the similarities, our individual stories remain distinctive.

It takes courage to ask the right questions to discover someone's story. It also takes courage to share your story with someone new. An amazing thing happens when two people of different backgrounds share their stories. When both choose to be vulnerable enough to reveal their pain, their struggles, and even their victories without judgment or criticism, those two human beings connect. When you accept someone as they are, you lay the foundation for relating—for having a relationship. I'm not talking about a romantic one but friendship, fellowship—*Koinonia*. This is a Greek word, meaning community, communion, joint participation, and intimacy.[1] When you share your true self and choose curiosity over criticism, you create a bond.

> **AN AMAZING THING HAPPENS WHEN TWO PEOPLE CHOOSE TO BE VULNERABLE ENOUGH TO REVEAL THEIR PAIN, THEIR STRUGGLES, AND EVEN THEIR VICTORIES WITHOUT JUDGMENT OR CRITICISM.**

THE ART OF CONNECTION

The trick is staying curious. We humans are people of habit. We move in and out of various interactions with people, usually so we can get to the next interaction. When you are at the grocery store, it's easy to see those who work there as just fixtures of the store. People doing a job. But they are people. My father-in-law was a master of curiosity. He wouldn't call himself that, but he never met a person he couldn't relate to. He'd always start up conversations with people he didn't know.

I have tried to emulate him sometimes. Sometimes, I just want to get my bread and ice cream and go home. But throughout our day, most of us encounter people who have stories. Curious people care enough to stop and get a piece of that story. Often, it takes time to be curious. It takes humility because to do this, particularly with strangers, you are sacrificing your precious time to esteem someone more highly than yourself. Since most of us fall prey to the clock, we don't always allow for the time to be curious.

Getting along with people takes time. It takes effort. It is an investment. Proverbs says, "To be a friend, you must be friendly."[2] This is such an obvious but full statement. Being friendly means you make time to ask curious questions (and actively listen to the answers) for your friends, family, and others you encounter.

CLARIFYING QUESTIONS

We also talked a bit about clarifying questions in "Learn to Listen." To actively listen will require that you ask clarifying questions. Those questions, though, should be phrased in ways that actually bring clarity.

ASK CURIOUS QUESTIONS

Many times, we try to ask questions to get more information to understand the speaker yet instead, the speaker reacts defensively. Why? Well, sometimes, clarifying questions sound like an interrogation.

You remember when you were sixteen and had that first taste of freedom. You just passed the driver's exam and waited somewhat impatiently for your license to come in the mail. It finally came, and you felt like a real driver. Sure, you could drive with that paper license, but when the real thing is in your hand, it just feels better. So then you start to march out the door toward the car, either your parents' minivan or the beat-up junker your dad got a great deal on. No sooner did you put your hand on the front door towards real freedom when your mom, or step-mom in my case, asks, "Where are you going?"

Ugh!

That's when the stream of other questions begins to pelt you like an automatic weapon: "Who are you going with?" "When will you be home?" "Why do you need to go now? It doesn't start for thirty minutes?" "Will there be adults there?" "How long will it take?" "Do you have your phone?"

All of those are clarifying questions. I have been the one to ask and been the one being asked. Being on the receiving end can feel like being under the interrogation lights at the police station (although I have never been there, I'm guessing what it feels like). As the parent, I just wanted to be sure that my kid would come back safely. As the sixteen-year-old, I just wanted to go hang out with my friends. But the questions that tried to bring clarity only caused conflict or, at the least, tension between parent and child.

THE ART OF CONNECTION

So, how do you ask clarifying questions that don't feel like you are accusing the other person?

First, you should avoid questions that begin with the word "Why." Anytime you use the word "why," it sounds like you accuse the other person of wrongdoing. Even the most innocent "why" feels like you question the intelligence or judgment of the receiver.

Asking "why" of yourself is great for reflection. When you point that "why" outward toward someone else, it creates a defensive response. "Why questions" are inherently accusatory. No matter the tone or situation, "why questions" feel like criticism. And, like we said before, *criticism kills relationships.*

So, how do you turn the accusatory question into a curious one? Begin with "What." Beginning your question with the word "what" will help you discover information that you didn't know before. Using the right words won't eliminate an accusatory tone; however, if you really do want to discover new information and are sincerely curious, beginning with "what" will help you get there.

If I ask someone, "Why did you think that would work?" I've made an accusation. If I ask, "What led you to make that decision?" I have begun a curious discussion. Especially if my intent really is to understand. You may also use "how" instead of "why," yet sometimes even how can seem accusatory.

> **PROBING QUESTIONS GET YOU FROM EVENTS AND FACTS TO FEELINGS AND MOTIVATIONS.**

These kinds of questions are probing questions. Questions that get into the deeper levels of truth and information. Questions that look into the intent of the heart rather than the shallow responses from defensive listeners.

ASK CURIOUS QUESTIONS

Probing questions get you from events and facts to feelings and motivations. Once you have clarity of facts, then the deeper questions can be asked. Of course, sometimes you might have to ask permission to ask these questions. It may not be the right time, or you may not have built up enough trust in the relationship to ask more probing questions.

PROBING QUESTIONS

Among the many types of questions we ask, I encourage using probing questions to find solutions to problems. Getting along with people means helping people with their problems. Although we want to help by suggesting solutions or giving advice, that's not the best way. In fact, that could exacerbate the problem and strain your relationship.

Instead, we should rely on the genius inside each person. When you see people as smart and capable, you don't feel the need to rescue them. That's where probing questions come in.

As a business owner, pastor, and leader, I prefer to use a coaching method of leadership as opposed to a command and control style of leadership. Command and control leaders use their positional authority to force you to do what they want. They tell you what to do, and you do it. It's a weak style of leadership that doesn't train your people to think for themselves and find solutions without you.

A company can have success with the command and control leader, yet that success will eventually find its cap or lid—it can only grow as far as the leader. When every decision requires the leader to make it, your organization will eventually stall. Until people are empowered to make decisions on their own, you won't grow. Craig Groeschel

THE ART OF CONNECTION

said, "You can have control, or you can grow, but you can't do both." At some point, you will have to shift decision-making downward.

That's where coaching leadership thrives. I'm not talking about coaching like your high school football coach who yelled at you, grabbed your face mask to get your attention, and made you run laps to punish you. No, I'm talking about business or life coaching that helps you become aware of things you may not see, understand your responsibility, and asks the right questions so you can find the solution on your own.

"So," you ask, "how does that relate to getting along with people if I'm not someone's life coach or their boss trying to reach some organizational goal?"

My answer to you is this: no, you aren't those things, yet the principles that the life coach and business coach use can make you a better friend, a better parent, spouse, employee, or employer. They can help you stay out of other people's business yet be there for them when they have issues.

Michael Bungay Stanier wrote *The Coaching Habit: Say Less, Ask More & Change the Way You Lead Forever*. It's a concise book on coaching and uses what he calls "The Seven Essential Questions" to help change your conversations and create a coaching habit.

As we go through these questions, I will show you how they relate to your everyday relationships.

The first question is the "kick-start" question to most coaching meetings. **"What's on your mind?"**

So Mike came into my office the other day. He's a friend as much as he is part of the team at the church where I was an associate pastor.

Ask Curious Questions

I could tell something was bothering him. Instead of letting him fester or ignoring the obvious, I asked him, "What's on your mind?"

That opened the door to our conversation. I came around my desk and sat nearby on the couch in my office. It wasn't job-related. It was personal. So, I didn't take notes. But, I did use many of the active listening techniques we discussed. I didn't try to solve his problem. I didn't tell him he shouldn't worry or just pray more. I listened. Where appropriate, I asked clarifying questions. But mostly, I encouraged him to talk.

"What's on your mind?" isn't one of the conversation starters we discussed earlier because I probably wouldn't use it with someone I just met. Some people ask, "What are you thinking?" That's not the same thing. Asking someone what they are thinking will rarely get an honest answer. The same as "Penny for your thoughts?" They seem intrusive. Asking someone what's on their mind says that you noticed they seem worried or preoccupied. And you're asking them if they want to talk about it. You can even ask that as well.

If someone has something on their mind, you might ask them, "Do you want to talk about it now? After work? Some other more appropriate time?" You are telling them with a question, "I am here for you if you want to talk about it."

The next question, called the "awe" question, **"And what else?"** Maybe they have talked for a while, yet they seem to be holding something back. Perhaps you just want them to keep talking. When people talk about their problems, it reduces their stress

WHEN PEOPLE TALK ABOUT THEIR PROBLEMS, IT REDUCES THEIR STRESS OR ANXIETY ABOUT THE ISSUE.

or anxiety about the issue. So, even if they talk in circles or repeat themselves as they process, just keeping someone talking with you actively listening helps them. It's called the "awe questions" because they seem so simple, yet they result in so much more depth.

As a friend, it's not your responsibility to solve all the world's problems. Nor is it to solve your friends and family's problems. When we talk about boundaries, we will discuss how not to take on other's problems. But with these probing questions, you may help your friends see the issue differently. As they talk their problem through, they may come up with solutions they didn't see before. Remember, coaching helps people become more aware. Awareness brings insight.

The "focus" question helps the person find clarity. **"What's the real challenge here?"** After talking through the issues and seeing from many different angles, your friend may see that their initial problem isn't the problem at all. Instead, there may be a deeper issue at the core. By asking the questions, you're helping your friend gain insight.

I had a friend who recently divorced and, aside from a small inheritance, didn't have a lot of financial resources. She hadn't worked outside the home since she started having kids. She needed a plan to create recurring income and provide housing for herself and her kids. While talking about her budget, where she was looking, and what her job options were, I asked her what she wanted. The conversation went to several different places after, but I kept going back to that question. **"What do you want?"** It's the foundation question.

ASK CURIOUS QUESTIONS

I have used that question in many coaching conversations. It's a shame how much we think about what we need to do. It's like the quote from the movie Gladiator, "Sometimes I do what I want to do, but most of the time I do what I must." Only from what I can see, many people aren't doing what they want. They were told that they should go to college. In order to get a good job, college is a must. Then, they needed to find a good job. Well, that was tough, but they think they found a job that paid well and had good benefits. Years down the road, they realized that they did everything to please other people, but nothing that pleased themselves.

I'm not talking about being a narcissist or a self-absorbed jerk. But doing things because it pleases others makes you a slave. Proverbs says, "Fear of man brings a snare, but trust in the Lord makes one safe."[3] The problem with trying to please others every day, all the time, is that at some point, you will get tired. Then, you will get bitter and resentful. Sometimes, you might even blame those people for your decisions.

> THE PROBLEM WITH TRYING TO PLEASE OTHERS EVERY DAY, ALL THE TIME, IS THAT AT SOME POINT, YOU WILL GET TIRED.

Thinking about what you want isn't a sin. It isn't wrong to want a job that you enjoy, not just a job that you are good at.

Once your friend has clarity, knows what the challenge is, and what they want to do about it, you may ask them, **"How can I help?"** Stanier calls this the "lazy" question. That's because the goal is to keep you lazy. When you ask, "How can I help?" you stop the rescue mode on the inside that wants to give advice and fix them. Instead, you are asking them to think of some way that you could help.

THE ART OF CONNECTION

Which, of course, you are ready to say either, "Yes, I can do that," or "No, I can't do that, but I could do ..." It's okay to say no. Saying no alerts others of your boundaries (which we will discuss later).

You can also defer by saying you need to think about it. Either way, you are asking your friend to think of solutions on their own. You might ask, **"What other things can you do to find a solution?"** before you ask the "How can I help?" question. After a few "And what else?" questions to exhaust the possible actions to take, your help may not be necessary.

Again, your goal is to stay out of other people's problems, inserting yourself where you don't belong. And yet, be a good friend.

The strategic question that Stanier asks is, **"What are you saying no to?"** Many people each January think about what they will do in the coming year. They make lists. Write down their goals (or at least they should). And while this is a great exercise to keep focused on your dreams, there's another list you should make. Jim Collins, in his book *Good to Great,* calls it your "Stop Doing List." This question is called the strategic question because *strategic planning is about choices.* Freedom is about having the power to choose. If you don't make choices, then you are a slave to the choices others make for you.

But you are not a slave. It is for freedom that Christ has set us free.[4] So we need to make two lists. A list of what you will do and another one of what you will say no to. In every decision, it is helpful to understand that when choosing a path, you are saying no to another or many other paths. If you choose to work late, you are choosing to say no to spending time with your family. If you choose to eat that cake, you are choosing to say no to better health (I don't

ASK CURIOUS QUESTIONS

believe having one piece of cake will harm you. I'm talking about consistent lifestyle choices). I once heard a pastor say that our power to choose is greater than God's power to plan. I'm not sure how I feel about that statement because I believe strongly in God's sovereignty. He's bigger than me, and His power is not dependent on my agency. Yet, I believe just as strongly that He gave us free will and expects us to exercise it. His nature indicates He allows the benefits and consequences of that free will to play out in the theater of time. Wherever the balance lies between God's plan and my choices, I know that I want to choose to stay on God's plans for my life.

> GOD'S NATURE INDICATES HE ALLOWS THE BENEFITS AND CONSEQUENCES OF OUR FREE WILL TO PLAY OUT IN THE THEATER OF TIME.

The last question that Stanier discusses is the learning question. **"What was most useful for you?"** Life consists of trial and error. Learning from victories and defeats. You, as a friend, might ask someone who has gone through a trial, **"What did you learn?"** This question normally comes at the end of a coaching session or a two-day seminar. The host may send out a survey that asks what most impacted you. But as friends and companions along life's journey should goad each other to reflect. At my last birthday dinner, I told my wife and kids that I wanted to start a new tradition. At each birthday dinner, we ask the person we are celebrating for words of wisdom they learned that year.

That wisdom may come from a book, the Bible, or some experience they had that year. For me, my birthday is in December. So, I get a calendar year look at life each year. But we all need to spend some time in self reflection. Whether in January or mid-summer. We should have friends around us who make us better. Who encourage us and ask us tough questions.

These curious, clarifying, probing questions not only help us through trials and issues, but they can help deepen and strengthen our relationships. That goes beyond just getting along.

ENDNOTES

1. *Koinōnia*. Strongs G2842. https://www.blueletterbible.org/lexicon/g2842/kjv/tr/0-1/
2. Proverbs 18:24, KJV.
3. Proverbs 29:25, ESV.
4. See Galatians 5:1.

ASK CURIOUS QUESTIONS

CHAPTER EIGHT DISCUSSION GUIDE

SUMMARY POINTS

- Curious questions communicate value and create connection by showing genuine interest in others' thoughts and stories.

- Asking the right questions builds self-awareness and opens the door to deeper understanding in relationships.

- Replacing "why" questions with "what" or "how" questions reduces defensiveness and encourages thoughtful conversation.

- Using coaching-style questions like "What's on your mind?" or "What do you want?" empowers others to find their own solutions.

- Cultivating curiosity requires humility, presence, and a willingness to invest time in discovering others' perspectives.

THE ART OF CONNECTION

DISCUSSION QUESTIONS • • • • • • • • • • •

1. How do you usually respond when someone shares a problem with you—do you give advice, ask questions, or something else?

2. Which curious question (from the chapter or your own experience) do you find most helpful in connecting with others?

3. What keeps you from asking deeper or more thoughtful questions in daily conversations?

4. In what ways could a coaching approach (asking more, telling less) benefit your relationships?

5. How can you grow in humility and curiosity in your conversations this week?

CHAPTER NINE

SET HEALTHY BOUNDARIES

THE BLUEPRINT FOR PROTECTING THE SPACE BETWEEN

Volumes have now been written on the subject of healthy boundaries. That is a good thing in many respects because they are so important for getting along with people. However, as people adopt the language of "healthy boundaries" in casual conversations without genuinely understanding what they are, how to set them, how to keep them, and the difference between a boundary and a wall, this becomes a barrier to healthy relationships. This brings us to the focus of this chapter: what are boundaries, and what makes them healthy?

Put simply; boundaries represent where we end, and others begin. Boundaries are the limitations we place on ourselves and others. Boundaries are good. Boundaries between countries can be free-flowing or guarded, but without boundaries, there can be no sovereignty. We have seen in the last few decades a great need to enforce a stronger boundary on our southern border. Why? Because not all those coming across into the United States have our best interests at heart. Without clearly established boundaries, you don't know who has authority over what territories or who is responsible for what. When the lines are blurred, misunderstandings between nations are guaranteed. The way we relate to people is very similar. Not everyone we let into our lives has our best interests at heart. Even those who do have the right motives may go about "enforcing" their ideas, rules, or limitations on us in ways that are harmful to us.

Boundaries protect your identity. Establishing and communicating boundaries is your responsibility.

In their book, *The Connection Codes: The Blueprint and Tools for Creating the Relationships You Crave*, Dr. Glenn and Phyllis Hill begin by sharing ways to protect and communicate your identity to others. Your identity searches for reinforcement that you exist, have value, are enough, and that you matter. When someone crosses a boundary, they harm your identity.

BOUNDARIES PROTECT AND PRESERVE YOUR HEART

Proverbs says, "Protect your heart, for out of it flows the issues of life."[1] Your heart is the seat of your identity, and boundaries protect your heart. Protecting your heart in relationships requires trust that other people will protect your heart also. That takes time and communicating clear boundary lines. Later I will share a story with you about my son, who didn't know that he crossed a boundary since that boundary had never been expressed.

So, how do you protect your heart without retreating from the world? For those who have been part of abusive relationships, your instinct is to draw back and withdraw from new relationships. But those are not boundaries—they are walls, and retreating behind them will rob you of life. Life flows from the connections we make with

SET HEALTHY BOUNDARIES

family, friends, co-workers, and church members. Letting people in after feeling betrayed or taken advantage of, or much worse, seems like a waste of time, a monumental risk without much reward.

But you can do it. You can protect your heart without withdrawing from the world. It begins by creating clear boundaries with those you love and who love you, saying no to the right things, and not taking on other people's problems.

Some people are takers. If you let them, they will take your time, energy, and resources for their own benefit. Jeff Vanvonderen defines abuse in his book, *Tired of Trying to Measure Up*, as one person using another person for their own benefit or to satisfy their own needs. It's a broad definition of abuse, yet helpful for us to identify areas that we need to protect ourselves. If you are in a relationship where another person, by intimidation, physical force, or under the guise of "spirituality," makes a habit of taking from you and using you to satisfy themselves, then learning to get along with them isn't the answer. Run away. Get out. Change jobs. Call the police. Whatever needs to be done to stop the abuse.

Abuse happens to people for many reasons. Sometimes, it starts from a lack of boundaries. Not everyone who crosses boundaries is an abuser, but every abuser begins by crossing subtle boundaries first. So, to have healthy relationships, we need to learn to set healthy boundaries.

When you begin to set boundaries, if they weren't there before, it will seem to those connected to you that

> **NOT EVERYONE WHO CROSSES BOUNDARIES IS AN ABUSER, BUT EVERY ABUSER BEGINS BY CROSSING SUBTLE BOUNDARIES FIRST.**

you are being rude, angry, or mean. That's okay. If someone isn't okay with your new boundaries, they weren't your friend in the first place. This book is about getting along with people—not being run over or pushed around by everyone. Instead, the goal for your relationships consists of healthy connections with people. Not one-sided parasite and host type of relationships.

What do I mean by a boundary? The other day, my son took my truck without asking permission. At the time, he and his wife lived with us. He drives one of my work vehicles, and since they had a baby, we have let them use one of our other vehicles as well. It was more suited for a growing family. When he took my truck, it really upset me. I didn't understand why for a few days. I even reacted with hostility when I needed it and he had put the keys somewhere I couldn't find them. Later, I realized why it upset me. He had crossed a boundary. Emotionally, when someone crosses a boundary, it feels like an attack on your identity. Like they ignored you, your agency, and your right to exist. Using other people's things without their permission says, "You don't matter to me."

Once I realized what the cause of my emotions was, I was able to forgive and move forward. I also realized that I hadn't set clear expectations around the use of my truck. In his mind, as my son, what's mine is his. That's the way it's been (or at least the way he thought it was) since before he was a teenager. If you don't know what your boundaries are, and if you have not taken the time to communicate that clearly, how can you expect them to know?

Like I said before, when boundaries are crossed, you may feel certain emotions. Angry, sad, hurt, etc. If the same boundary is crossed over and over again, you develop an emotional callous. You become numb in that area. You have lost your identity in that space.

SET HEALTHY BOUNDARIES

LINES THAT LIBERATE

> *"The boundary lines have fallen for me in pleasant places; surely I have a delightful inheritance."*
>
> PSALM 16:6, NIV

This Psalm of David expresses his trust and confidence in the Lord as he asks for protection. While this specific verse refers literally to land boundaries and David's inheritance from the Lord, it also expresses the boundaries set in place around David's life and experience and the inheritance of spiritual blessings, peace, and joy that God provides from living within those boundary lines. They are lines that liberate!

We are *meant* to have pleasure in our relationships. So, the first thing about setting clear boundaries is **knowing where to put them.** Then, you must let others know where they are. I don't mean like putting it in your newsletter, but when the occasion arises. For instance, you may have the boundary of not riding in the car with anyone who isn't your spouse. You don't need to put that on your Instagram, but if someone asks for a ride, you can tell them about your boundary.

So, practically, how do you function with boundaries where they weren't before?

Look at the areas where you have been hurt, where you felt like people ignored your identity or crossed a boundary. What happened?

What might have been the outcome if you had defined a boundary in this area and communicated it to others?

THE ART OF CONNECTION

Now, look at areas where you may have crossed someone else's boundaries. What happened?

How might the outcome have been different if you had known their boundaries?

This exercise should help you find out what your boundaries are. It may even help you recognize where someone else's boundaries ought to be—even if they have not stated them. (Awareness is such a beautiful thing!) The difficulty comes in trying to enforce them. Many people stress over other people's lives and choices. Control is an illusion. If you try to control someone else by fear or intimidation, you've crossed a line.

BOUNDARIES CREATE CHOICES

When you think of how God started this whole thing out, you see Him put two people in a garden filled with great fruit trees, and maybe there was a beach nearby. You know, it was paradise—and how could it be paradise without a beach? Only God didn't *just* put trees that were good for us there. He gave us the opportunity to make a choice. Good or bad, He created us with the power of choice. He loves us enough to let us make bad choices, even when He knows the consequences in advance—if He didn't, it wouldn't be love. It would be control. There would be no boundary granting us autonomy and allowing us to exercise free will and have the opportunity to choose Him ... or not.

When we trust God with other people, we have to be willing to let them make choices, even if they make a bad choice.

Danny Silk has a great book on parenting, *Loving Our Kids On Purpose,* where he explains that kids have the power to make good

SET HEALTHY BOUNDARIES

decisions if you let them. He talks about how you must give them the space to make those decisions. It is easy to see the consequences of not allowing children to make choices while they are under the protection of their parents. As they get older, they have never exercised that muscle, and they are paralyzed. They don't know how to make a decision, and their identity is stunted because making choices is a huge part of knowing who you are.

If you live a life without boundaries, you may be taking on the responsibilities of others around you and robbing them of the opportunity to make their own choices. I find it much easier to get along with people when I'm not trying to make their decisions for them.

When I decided to trust the Holy Spirit, who lives in my kids, instead of trying to influence them and give them my opinions all the time, we got along so much better. Let me tell you, it was not easy holding back my opinions when they spoke of the issues going on in their life. I am a fixer. So, I instinctively want to work on a solution to fix their problems.

My daughter, Kate, came to work for us because we lived in another town and needed someone to manage our real estate. I was desperate, and she was available. In hindsight, I believe she may have taken the job out of loyalty or some feeling like she had to please me. She was great at it, but we both could see that it was draining her of her joy. At the time, I was happy for her to be there. She was learning some skills that most people her age wouldn't have had the opportunity to acquire.

Now, I can see that when my kids work for me, it creates a different dynamic in our relationship. The boundary we saw crossed over and over was family vs. employee/employer. Family time turned into work discussions. Then, at work, I saw my kid instead of an employee. I learned that I was part of the problem. I didn't create distinct lines for each role. Kate decided to resign and take a job at a bank.

I wasn't happy about the decision at first, but now I see it was the right one. I decided then that I needed to trust God with my kids. I've made that decision in countless other areas, but for their financial, career, and other similar decisions, I had to let go. I'm not their provider anymore. My wife and I have used an expression to discuss this process. We call it "cutting the cord"—that would be the umbilical cord that supplies life to a baby while it's in the womb. It's a coarse expression we use to remind us to let go.

Having healthy boundaries requires that we let them make decisions for themselves.

EXTREME BOUNDARIES FOR EXTREME SITUATIONS

Sometimes, boundaries need to be extreme. We talked before about the definition of abuse: when you are in a relationship that uses you up and takes your energy, time, resources, innocence, and personhood. If this is the case, then the only thing to do is escape. You don't owe the abuser any explanation.

Abusers don't always know that they are abusers. Sometimes, they are narcissists who see everyone around them as a tool for their ambition. Narcissism is defined as a person who has an excessive interest in or admiration of themselves. Narcissists don't have boundaries when it comes to other people. They see any disagreement as disloyalty or even rebellion. They bring people in by being kind, and they give enough encouragement to keep them around. But if

SET HEALTHY BOUNDARIES

you cross them, they retaliate with accusations and criticism. When you walk away from them, they will see it as a betrayal and usually work hard to discredit you, 1. to yourself (by gaslighting), and 2. to others (smear campaign).

Not all abusers are narcissists, and not all narcissists are abusers. However, when you encounter these characteristics in one person, you should run the other way. There are many types of abusers: 1. Physical/Sexual abusers, 2. Emotional/Verbal abusers, 3. Spiritual abusers.

For abuse, the only way out is to escape, even if that means calling the authorities.

COMMUNICATING "YOU CROSSED THE LINE"

But only extreme cases require extreme boundaries. I want to discuss how you confront someone who merely crosses one of the boundaries you have set.

There must be consequences to those who trespass. If we respond with punishment, intimidation, or ultimatums, we make ourselves cross boundaries in others' lives. **We should focus on what we can control—ourselves.** What we can do is change our behavior or response. Remember that the idea that you can control other people is an illusion. Healthy consequences look more like withdrawing from the situation—ending a conversation, taking a break, or limiting contact. It involves communicating your feelings and needs and expressing what is no longer acceptable. It definitely requires setting reasonable, fair, and clear guidelines for future interactions.

Let's go back in time. Suppose I had told my son from the beginning, "Hey, I would appreciate it if you would not take my truck without asking first." That states a clear expectation of the boundary. He would have known my expectations, and he might never have driven it without checking with me first. But if he did, what should I do in return? Threaten him? Yell at him? That would strain our relationship. Instead, I might first communicate, "Son, when you took my truck without asking, it bothered me a lot. It meant I had to make alternative plans that were inconvenient for me. That is just not acceptable, and it can't happen again. If it does, you'll lose the privilege of access."

That is pretty clear communication of 1. My thoughts and feelings, expressing why it is important to me, and 2. The consequences of violating that boundary again.

So, let's say he is pretty thick-headed about it and decided to do it again? Well, I could decide to keep the keys with me, even if I use a different car. I could lock the truck keys in my room, where he would have to ask for them before using the vehicle. Those are things I could do without straining our relationship or threatening to take him out of the will.

Helping him become aware of my feelings in the first place would likely eliminate the need for other measures entirely. If my son also wants to protect the relationship, then he is likely to be repentant and respect my boundary going forward.

THE FREEDOM OF NO

One area that many people have trouble with is saying no. Saying no isn't mean or rude or selfish. It merely establishes a boundary or reinforces a boundary that you have already set. I was asked to teach a class at church a while back. While I love teaching and had

SET HEALTHY BOUNDARIES

done that class before, I had taken on other responsibilities that already took one or two evenings away from my family. Family time is a priority for me. I didn't want to say no, but I knew I had to. I realized that I had been stressing about telling the person who asked about my decision. Finally, I told them I couldn't teach the class that month. He said, "Okay, Thank you." And that was it. In my mind, I had made it out to be a bigger decision than it actually was.

Here are some healthy ways to communicate a "no" answer to people.

- **Be clear and direct.** Resist the urge to be vague, "I'll think about it and get back to you." Instead, "No, thank you, I am unable to do that." Note: no apologies are needed when you say no to a request.

- **You can be polite and even explain if you desire.** "Thank you for thinking of me, but I have other commitments that keep me from …"

- **Communicate your boundaries, even if this requires you to repeat a "no" when pressured.** You can calmly identify what you are and are not willing to do.

- **Remember, how they feel about your "no" is not in your control.** You do not need to accept guilt.

RETURN TO SENDER—DON'T ACCEPT SOMEONE ELSE'S PROBLEMS AS YOUR OWN

Taking on other people's problems robs them of the opportunity to be creative and possibly learn from their failures. There are many reasons people carry other people's burdens. You may love someone, like your kids, and don't want them to encounter the same trials and tribulations that you endured. You forget that those trials made you strong and created the success you currently enjoy.

I love the example Dr. Henry Cloud gave in his book *Boundaries*. There was a couple who had a son with a drug problem and had been kicked out of several schools. They listed several things they had done to "help" their son, but it didn't seem to phase him. They said their kid didn't think he had any problems. Dr. Cloud told them he agreed with the son. That shocked them. He told them that they were enabling their son by rescuing him over and over. He finally asked if they would like help giving their son some problems. You may need to give others back their problems.

You may be manipulated by someone who uses your love, your gifts, and your need to feel needed to serve their goals or needs (also defined as abuse). There are selfish people out there who seem to be drawn to those vulnerable to their schemes.

Several years ago, my mother moved to the town where we lived. She was in her late fifties and didn't qualify for social security yet. I own several houses as rentals and set her up in a small two-bedroom house. I furnished it and paid all the bills, including the telephone. Since she was healthy and able to work, I only asked that she pay $200 per month for rent. The fair value of the rent for that house, unfurnished without paying bills at the time, was $500 per month. I didn't need the $200. I just wanted her to have some responsibility and the dignity of paying part of her own way. I told her, though, that if she didn't pay the $200, we would evict her. Maybe that seems harsh to you. Yet, my history with my mother showed me she believed she was entitled to be taken care of. Looking back, now I believe that she had narcissistic personality disorder (NOD). As a narcissist, she

SET HEALTHY BOUNDARIES

believed that everyone owed her something. This, for me, was the last attempt at a battered and beaten relationship with my mom. If she would just stay consistent with a job and pay her minimal rent, I was open to connecting again—with boundaries.

It wasn't six months later, around Christmas, our kids received several hundred dollars of presents from her. Presents we knew she couldn't afford. And the following month, she didn't pay her rent. I asked her about the rent. She said she didn't have it, and she had quit her job. I couldn't believe what I was hearing. She was trying to make her problems my problem. Angela and I decided that we weren't going to receive her problems. I began the eviction process.

I didn't see or hear from my mother for at least thirteen years after that fiasco. I did hear from her sister, my aunt. She called to yell at me for evicting my own mother. Then, I explained what I did for her and what my mother did in return. She said, "Oh," and she didn't complain to me any longer. There are just some people who try to make their problems become your problems.

But we have to be wise as serpents and harmless as doves. I never stopped loving my mother. I chose not to give her access to our lives or let her try to manipulate me by shame and guilt trips into taking on her problems.

You can confront people in love. You can lovingly tell them no. You can, in love, empathize with their problems. And, in love, allow them the dignity of managing their problems.

> **YOU CAN LOVINGLY TELL PEOPLE NO WHILE EMPATHIZING WITH THEM AND ALLOWING THEM THE DIGNITY OF MANAGING THEIR OWN PROBLEMS.**

THE ART OF CONNECTION

Healthy boundaries are the foundation of thriving relationships. You can't get along with people for very long without them. Boundaries are necessary with family, at work, at church, and anywhere else you encounter humans. Healthy boundaries create clarity, foster respect, and lay the foundation for the kind of trust you need to experience genuine human connection and growth in relationships. Boundaries protect your heart—they preserve your identity. When you take the time to define your boundaries and communicate them clearly, it protects your mental and emotional well-being. Walking inside the safety of healthy boundaries allows you to flourish as a human being, grounded, resilient, and connected.

ENDNOTE

1. Proverbs 4:23, paraphrased.

SET HEALTHY BOUNDARIES

CHAPTER NINE
DISCUSSION GUIDE

SUMMARY POINTS

- Boundaries define where you end and others begin. They protect your identity, your time, and your emotional space.

- Healthy boundaries clarify your responsibilities and expectations without trying to control others.

- Saying "no" with clarity and confidence is essential for maintaining your limits and well-being.

- There's a difference between building walls and setting boundaries—walls isolate, while boundaries preserve connection and identity.

- In abusive or manipulative situations, strong boundaries—even separation—are necessary to restore safety and dignity.

THE **ART** OF **CONNECTION**

DISCUSSION QUESTIONS • • • • • • • • • •

1. What's one area of your life where your boundaries are too weak or unclear, and how is it affecting you?

2. Have you ever confused a wall for a boundary? What was the result in that relationship?

3. How do you typically respond when someone crosses a boundary you've set (or should have set)?

4. What's one way you can begin practicing the power of saying "no" without guilt?

5. How can setting clearer boundaries actually lead to stronger, more respectful relationships?

CHAPTER TEN

THE END ... AND THE REAL BEGINNING

JR. HIGH PICK-UP ARTIST

When I was in junior high (that's middle school to some of you), I developed a five-step process to meet girls. I know—I was a genius then, too. Honestly, it worked pretty well for me, so maybe it will help you. I shared this with one of my friends and saw him go from a Transformer-carrying sixth grader to a highly popular eighth grader. Of course, it could also have been his athletic abilities and hitting puberty, but we may never know. How does this apply to this book? I can't exactly tell you that I know, but this kind of gold needs to be shared ...

- **STEP 1. Eye contact.** The meet-cute in all good romantic stories always begins with eye contact. That look across the room. The deep stare. The startled, "Oh, I'm so sorry I bumped into you .." It's the beginning of the relationship that lets them know you exist.

THE ART OF CONNECTION

- **STEP 2. Say their name.** People like to hear their names in conversations. Use their name as much as you can without sounding weird. Saying their name lets them recognize that you know they exist.

- **STEP 3. Be around them.** Find ways to be in the same room. Sign up for the same class, go to the same movie, same basketball game, ... This step is all about proximity. Also, keep up with steps one and two.

- **STEP 4. Inadvertent physical touch.** Really, this is just an expansion of step three. While you are in the same room, stand close so your shoulders can rub against each other. Sit close while watching a game. These steps sound so corny now. But hey, I was thirteen and thought I knew everything.

- **STEP 5. Smile every time you see them, talk to them, or make eye contact with them.** This step assumes that you have already begun talking to them on a regular basis. It also may have heavily relied upon my dimpled cheeks. Teenage girls and grandmas alike love kids with dimples.

What's great about this list that I thought was a breakthrough in getting girls to notice me, is that it's really just a process where people become friends. Unfortunately, my skills in getting girls' attention didn't translate into creating long-lasting relationships. That's what this book is for. I promise it was *not* for dating advice but rather how to cultivate long-lasting, high-quality, meaningful relationships. How to get along with anyone, anywhere.

Many of us have the same issue I had in junior high. Starting relationships may be easy for some, but keeping relationships

THE END AND THE REAL BEGINNING

challenges us all. When I was younger, I had maybe five "best" friends. There were years that my "best" friend changed each year because the school I went to was so large that I might not see my friends all day, forcing me to make new friends.

As the years have passed, I held on to one or two close friends. The others lost touch due to moves, college, marriages, and kids. In the early childhood years, we sought friends who also had kids. As our kids grew up, we noticed that our friend pool had decreased to nearly nothing. For most of that, I accept the responsibility. I put my job and career goals above everything and everyone. Sometimes, I would break the relationship with people because they didn't fit into my plans. As I said before, I was not a likable person.

The principles in this book can help you avoid my mistakes. I hope reading it has transformed your thinking and made you more aware of the value of others. I look back on those who have come and gone and realize that I missed out on the true treasure. Jesus said that if we are faithful in little things, we will be trusted with true riches. Those true riches walk around us every day. Everyone has a story, and everyone's story has value. I regret not taking the time to recognize this truth earlier in life.

YOU CAN NOW MOVE ABOUT THE CABIN

> *"Ladies and gentlemen, you have completed all chapters of this book, and you have reached cruising altitude in your understanding. The seatbelt sign has been turned off, and you are now free to move about the cabin."*

By now you are an expert on interpersonal relationships and will be able to easily move about your life with ease.

THE ART OF CONNECTION

Or maybe not.

Maybe you are like me and still have to work on getting along with people. Knowing how to do something and putting it into practice are very different things. I wrote this book so that you could start sooner in life than I did at realizing your role in having meaningful relationships with people.

Remembering what Paul said, "As much as depends on you, live peaceably ..."[1] I spent years blaming others for breaking relationships with me. It wasn't until I became aware of my habits of criticism, self-centeredness, lack of curiosity, and poor listening skills that I realized that much of the brokenness in my relationships depended on me.

> **IT'S OKAY IF YOU MAKE MISTAKES. JUST CORRECT THEM IN THE MOMENT YOU REALIZE THEM AND MOVE ON.**

When you do become aware, it can be very easy to draw back and be hesitant to start new relationships. Awareness, though, should lead to trying things a new way. Hopefully, this book can be a compass. It can help you feel better about getting along with people in general. And it's okay if you make mistakes. Just correct them in the moment you realize them and move forward.

Nobody expects you to be an expert at interpersonal relationships.

Even after reading this book. God knows that I am not an expert. I still have trouble navigating conversations and listening to people for understanding instead of just waiting to respond. I wrote this book

THE END AND THE REAL BEGINNING

as a testament to my failures. As a way to identify my weaknesses and find solutions for them.

Remember, we live by grace through faith. We believe that God is working in us and through us. And that the work He began, He is faithful and just to complete it. This book isn't meant to spotlight your deficiencies or condemn you. I wrote this book to help spark your curiosity to get to the root of why things in your relationships might not be the way you desire them. I hope sharing my journey helps you find new self-awareness. I urge you to allow the Holy Spirit to continue to bring the fruit of the Spirit in you.

Whose relationships wouldn't benefit from the intentional growth and development of love, joy, peace, patience, kindness, goodness, gentleness, and self-control?

RELATIONSHIP CLIFFNOTES

We began this book by discussing what it means to get along. Deciding who we will spend our energy on and allow our peace to rest with. Once we decide who warrants our time, energy, and peace, we then learned how to begin the process of, as much as it depends on us, living peaceably with people.

- **Avoid Criticism:** In the first step, we learned to avoid criticism. I know I have said it many times, but criticism kills relationships. If you only remember one thing from that chapter, I hope it's that one truth you take away. As much as you think you are helping to solve your friend's problems, when you are critical, all they hear from you is how much they fall short. Be more aware of what you say to others and how they may take your "great" advice.

THE ART OF CONNECTION

- **Praise Freely:** Next we get into the more positive steps in the process. Praising freely means to encourage others. Build them up instead of tearing them down. Acknowledge their strengths. Pour courage into those around you!

- **Express Appreciation:** Next to encouragement, there is appreciation. A language of its own, appreciation can be expressed in many ways. Not everyone speaks the same appreciation or love language. Learn the love language of your friends, family, and others so you can truly express your appreciation in a way they can receive it.

- **Forgive Quickly:** Of course, we have opportunities every day to be offended, hold grudges, and keep our relationships in debt to us. But if we choose to forgive quickly, we free ourselves from the bondage of that debt. Not condoning wrong behavior or allowing others to hurt us at will, but making sure that our hearts stay free from bitterness, we forgive. We let go.

- **Listen Actively:** Another active step in getting along requires us to learn to listen actively. Listening isn't a passive activity. To truly listen and engage, you need to provide feedback, ask questions, and maybe take notes. Depending on the circumstances, listeners have the responsibility to engage in communication. Don't be a hearer only.

- **Ask Probing Questions:** When engaged in conversations or new situations with new people, asking probing questions deepens the conversation and tells those you want to get along with that you care and that you are curious to know more about them and the subject of the conversation. We

THE END AND THE REAL BEGINNING

looked at a few lists of questions that help you get more out of your conversations while avoiding trying to fix your friends' issues.

O **Set Healthy Boundaries:** Finally, we learned about having healthy boundaries—the boundaries that protect your identity. Boundaries establish where others end, and you begin. Boundaries not only keep bad feelings out, but they also protect your voice from within.

WHICH WAY FORWARD FROM HERE

> *"So then faith comes by hearing and hearing by the Word of God."*
>
> ROMANS 10:17

I'm not saying that this book is the Word of God. But I'd like you to think about the implications of the above verse. You can believe something only after you hear it and know it. Further, you can only act once you have become aware. (Faith without works is dead.[2]) As I have quoted in other books, "Which way forward from here?"

Now that you are aware, what steps will you take?

What will you do with the information read in the previous chapters?

Will you believe?

Will you act?

Will you transform?

THE **ART** OF **CONNECTION**

I hope so. I hope that you will, like me, evaluate your life and behavior. Allow the Holy Spirit to guide you into all truth. Not just the truth that you agree with. I didn't want to believe that I was critical. I only wanted to help people. I only wanted to use my superior wisdom and intellect to help all the lowly minions around me. *Did we talk about pride before?* That was harsh, I know. But sometimes we have to be shocked into change!

We all have had many goals and dreams over the years. They change as we have changed. We are all evolving. I don't believe in the theory of evolution, but I do believe in the evolving of our souls.

We are all on a journey to find our true selves. The one whom God created us to become. The best version of ourselves already lives. We have been made a new creation in Christ. That born-again spirit has all the attributes and character of Jesus. We just need to allow Christ in us, the hope of glory, to live through us.

So now that you have this book, you can become more aware of others' needs. You can allow the Holy Spirit to work through you to get along with others.

As much as it depends on you, live peaceably with all ...

Get out there and start getting along.

ENDNOTE

1. See Romans 12:18, ESV.

Our born-again spirit has all the attributes and character of Jesus, so the best version of ourselves already lives. We just need to allow Christ in us, the hope of glory, to live through us.

About the Author

Brandon Moore is a CPA, Certified Wealth Strategist©, coach, and real estate investor with a passion for helping people grow—not just financially, but relationally. Through decades of advising clients, building businesses, and mentoring leaders, he's seen that true success hinges on our ability to connect and communicate well.

Alongside his wife of almost thirty years, Brandon has raised four children, managed over a hundred properties, and built a family-centered life rooted in faith, integrity, and personal growth. He shares his insights through coaching, books, and speaking.

When he's not working, Brandon enjoys making music at church and training in Taekwondo, where he holds a third-degree black belt.

Connect with Brandon at:

WWW.BRANDONKMOORE.COM

MORE BOOKS FROM BRANDON K. MOORE

THE BEGINNING OF WEALTH

Brandon Moore reveals the 7 Wealth Behaviors that ordinary people—teachers, entrepreneurs, tradespeople—can use to build extraordinary financial legacies. Grounded in the Entrepreneur Hero's Journey, this book will help you take control of your future, redefine success, and create a life that aligns with your purpose.

THE E-HERO'S JOURNEY

This book reframes entrepreneurship as a transformational adventure, filled with purpose, risk, and growth. With practical wisdom and real-life examples, this book equips you to face challenges, rise above fear, and become the hero of your own business story.

THE E-HERO'S GUIDE TO REAL ESTATE INVESTING

This book is a practical, story-driven roadmap for entrepreneurs looking to build passive income and lasting wealth through real estate. With real-life lessons, honest insights, and step-by-step guidance, Brandon Moore shows you how to invest wisely, grow steadily, and create freedom on your terms.

AVAILABLE ON AMAZON.COM

Made in the USA
Coppell, TX
24 December 2025

65304180R00095